# Old Testament Story

## Seeing the Old Testament as a whole.

by

**AUDREY NASH**

authorHOUSE®

AuthorHouse™ UK Ltd.
500 Avebury Boulevard
Central Milton Keynes, MK9 2BE
www.authorhouse.co.uk
Phone: 08001974150

First published by AuthorHouse 10/27/2008

ISBN: 978-1-4389-2873-9 (sc)

Printed in the United States of America
Bloomington, Indiana

This book is printed on acid-free paper.

# Contents

# *Introduction*

"COME ON," SAID MY FRIEND, "Let's face it, the Old Testament is really old bilge, isn't it?" This was said to me well over thirty years ago when I was studying theology. The view expressed to me by this friend, a fellow member of a little estate church, was then, and is now, a widespread opinion.

There have been occasions in my life when I am glad that I often react slowly and that was one of them!

Sadly nowadays the Old Testament is a closed book to the majority of people in this country. So my hope is that this little book will encourage you to dig into it yourself. But let me warn you from my own experience. Once you do really get into the Old Testament, you won't want to get out of it. Here is something which is addictive and good for you at the same time!

❧

I recently read a fascinating book about a study done on what makes a good wildlife garden under the title, "No Nettles Required". The author, Ken Thompson, pointed out that, while there are plenty of books on the subject, there had been remarkably little research. What was happening was that authors were merely repeating untested theories

1

as to what makes a garden good for wildlife. Yet many of these much quoted theories are simply untrue. That is exactly what happens with the Old Testament. People are too often content merely to repeat what they have heard about it without testing whether or not their adopted opinion is supported by the evidence.

Sadly even Christians are willing to express an opinion about it based on hearsay and ignorance. I would maintain one's right to a valid opinion about a book is established only at the price of reading the whole book thoroughly. That is not unreasonable, is it? But it applies to the Old Testament as much as to anything else.

✥

Many claim that they are appalled at the violence in the Old Testament. Further the god found there is really quite a nasty piece of work. Vengeful and vindictive, he is only too ready to jump on people when they put the least foot wrong. The New Testament fortunately is quite different, as all you will find there is just love.

If, after you have read the Old Testament, covering as it does fifteen hundred years of human history, you find that the violence there still worries you, I have one suggestion to make which will give you a sense of proportion. Read Tom Holland's splendidly written book, "Rubicon" about the Roman Republic. You will come away from that realising how restrained and mild the people in the Old Testament were compared with the Romans. And we are usually taught to look up to the Romans. Can't think why! Now they really were a bloodthirsty lot.

Happily the nasty Old Testament god of much Christian imagining does not exist. We are going to have a look through the Old Testament and so will get some idea what the God revealed there is like. There is, of course, only one way to get the full picture and you can already guess what that is! Read it for yourself. In fact God does not go off-stage between the testaments and do a character change as many people fondly imagine. The God of both testaments is the same: righteous, holy and just, the God of salvation, grace, love and mercy and compassion. But yes, He certainly is more fully revealed through Jesus Christ in the New Testament.

For years I tutored Old Testament courses for the London School of Theology, formerly London Bible College. The result was that I found myself explaining the same aspects of the Old Testament time and again. This re-inforced my conviction that there was a need for an easily read account of the whole Old Testament story to enable readers to see how it all fits together. So here goes!

An Ulster Protestant student of mine wrote that as a result of her upbringing she thought God was a distant heavy handed Judge, waiting to catch you out every time you stepped out of line.

She answered an essay question entitled, "What impact has your study of the Old Testament had on your Christian faith?"

She wrote, "I began to relax in my relationship with God and to stop feeling guilty all the time." Did you get that? It was from reading the Old Testament that this person found she could begin to relax in her relationship with God! Try it!

❧

As you well know, the Bible is divided into two parts which are the Old Testament and the New Testament. Another word for 'testament' here is the word 'covenant'. You will understand why that is so before long. The New Testament is built on the Old Testament and it cannot be understood adequately without it. But the Old Testament is not just a mine for proof texts fulfilled in the New Testament. It also has a great value in itself. There are riches here worth discovering. Great truths are taught here which are assumed rather than repeated in the New

Testament. Much of the modern church has lost sight of some of these and, as a result, it is vastly impoverished. .

The impact of the Old Testament can only be appreciated when it is seen as a whole. Seeing the Old Testament as a whole simply does not happen in modern church life. I have been in various churches for well over fifty years now. The only occasions when I have come across any attempt to help folk in church to see the Old Testament as a whole and grasp how it all hangs together have been in the few courses I have had the opportunity of running myself! So one of the purposes of this book is to bridge that gap and let you see how the Old Testament all fits together. But the main purpose for which I write is to encourage you to read the Old Testament for yourself and so allow God to speak to you through it, as He surely will if you just give Him the opportunity. Perhaps that is what He is waiting for.

The Old Testament contains 39 books written in Hebrew, which was the language of the Israelites. (There are just a couple of passages written in Aramaic). Some books are quite long, some very short indeed. They were written without the chapter and verse divisions with which we may be familiar. These were added for convenience a great deal later. Handy though these are for finding a particular passage and for referring to it, they were often put in places where they hinder one seeing the sense of the whole passage. So when reading just for one's own benefit it can often pay one to ignore them.

Apart from the first eleven chapters of Genesis, the Old Testament books cover a period of just over 1500 years from Abraham to Malachi, that is, from somewhere near 2000 BC to around 450 BC.

As we read the Old Testament we first need to ask, "What did the writer mean in the Ancient Near Eastern context in which he lived?" Only when we have answered that question can we begin to see what it has to say to us. It does have a great deal to say to us! One lady, who was reading the Old Testament through for perhaps the first time, exclaimed, "The people in it are just like us!" Indeed they are.

By the way the area called the Ancient Near East in Bible times is now the Middle East! Sorry I can't tell you how it slipped from being near to middle. I'd like to know.

# Setting the Scene: Genesis 1-11

AT FIRST THERE WAS ONLY God. There always had been God. He made everything else that there is. He did not need to do this, but He freely chose that it should be so. It all happened on His initiative and by His power. So it is all His. Because it is all God's handiwork, something of the Creator is revealed through it.

But everything around us is not God, nor is it part of God. That is an important distinction, because in some Eastern religions all that exists is part of the god. No, God, the Creator, is quite separate from His creation. Thus, being in that sense, outside it, He can do new things in it and through it. He can order it as He will. He could get on very well without any of it, but like it or not, creation cannot get on at all without Him.

We do not read about God as Creator only in the first couple of chapters of Genesis. This is a significant theme also in the prophetic books, the Psalms and the book of Job as well as occurring elsewhere in the Old Testament. Interestingly enough the Old Testament has no word equivalent to our 'Nature', that lady who does her own thing. This is because it is all God's creation and so it does not do its own thing.

At first it was all very good and humanity was included in that evaluation.

But that is not how we experience the world now. So what happened to change it? What went wrong?

God had created humans innocent but with the potential of choosing good or evil. For humans to be moral beings, to be good or evil or a mixture of the two, there must be a choice for them to make. God provided for them abundantly but He also gave them the command, "... of the fruit of the tree of the knowledge of good and evil you shall not eat" (Genesis 2:16 ESV) Here it is important to note that the word for 'knowledge' in the Old Testament is often nearer in meaning to our word 'experience'. So the way the human pair responded to this command would result in their experiencing good or evil according to their choice.

But the man and woman chose to disobey this command with catastrophic results. Mind you, have you ever thought that if the Old Testament god were anything like the creature of most peoples' imagining, then he would have simply wiped humans off the earth there and then. In that case you would not be where you are at this moment reading this book?

What were the immediate results of this disobedience?

The man and woman hid from the Lord God because they had fractured their relationship with Him by their disobedience. They no longer felt comfortable with Him; they no longer enjoyed His Presence.

God gave them the opportunity to face up to what they had done. However, when He questioned them, their replies were not very promising. The man put the blame for his own action on both the woman and on God. After all, he was not going to take responsibility for what he had done. (Sounds remarkably modern, doesn't it?) "The woman whom

8

you gave to be with me, she gave me fruit of the tree, and I ate". (Genesis 3:12 ESV)

The woman didn't do much better: she blamed the serpent. The relationship between the human pair was fouled up, as each was seeking to pass the blame elsewhere.

The environment too was spoiled. Sin, human wrongdoing, disobedience to God is the reason why so much is awry in this world.

❧

Incidentally then, we are wrong when we excuse ourselves by saying that our failing at any particular point was simply due to our human nature. The Genesis story makes it clear that sin's place in human nature is that of an invader, not a native. This is critically important and widely misunderstood. Yes, sin has penetrated the nature of each one of us, but it does not belong there. One day, as recorded in the New Testament, there came One Who was fully human, (as well as fully God) and yet without sin. That would not have been possible if sin were an essential part of being human.

❧

Almost immediately we read of the growth of human wickedness. In the next generation, Cain murders Abel his brother. After that things go from bad to worse.

❧

The story of Noah and the ark and the flood is not just a nice children's story, though it is too often treated as such. It is a terrifying story of the kind of judgement which human wickedness deserves.

By Noah's time we read of humanity that "Every intention of the thoughts of his heart was only evil continually " (Genesis 6:5 ESV) That was indeed a sorry state of affairs. God judges human wickedness. But in the midst of judgement there was also salvation, that is deliverance or rescue, for the man and his family who responded to God.

In God's choice of Noah  do notice that Genesis 6:8 comes before Genesis 6:9 (Most Christians don't see that!) Verse 8 tells us that Noah finds favour in God's eyes and verse 9 informs us that he is a blameless man. It works that way round in both testaments. A relationship with God has God's grace or favour as its basis and so it leads to a life of integrity. If it doesn't, then one is entitled to question the reality of the relationship.

God uses His own creation to bring judgement by means of a flood. His creation is at His command. After this He makes a covenant agreement with Noah, with his descendants and with every living creature, that a flood of such proportions would not recur.

❧

The building of the Tower of Babel illustrates humanity's pride and bid for independence from God and it too reaps judgement. Pride and independence remain our besetting sins, along with selfishness, and we can learn a great deal about them, (and about ourselves,) in the Old Testament!

So Genesis 1-11 introduces some of the major OT themes: creation, sin, judgement, grace, (that is, God's undeserved love, generosity and favour), and salvation, (rescue, deliverance, initiated and carried out by God). It also makes it clear that this is God's world.  For if He were not Creator, if it all somehow just happened on its own, then He would be an intruder. For the whole of the Bible, Old Testament as well as New, by definition God is the Almighty Creator of all that there is. You cannot have more than one of them. Thus as C. S. Lewis pointed out, God, rightly understood, is a word with no plural. Other gods are mere humans writ large, or else the personification of some aspect of creation.

⊷

Thus the opening chapters of the Bible introduce us to a disastrous situation with humanity in rebellion against God. God was not taken by surprise. He already knew what He would do about it. So He takes the initiative to begin to deal with all this.

# The Patriarchs:
# Genesis 11:27-50:26.

WE COME TO THE PATRIARCHS who are Abraham, Isaac, Jacob and
his twelve sons. The word 'patriarch' comes from two Greek words,
one meaning 'father' and the other 'ruler'. Thus the patriarchs are the
father-rulers. Each was in turn head of his own clan, centred around his
extended family, along with its servants. But as Genesis 14:14 shows us,
this could be a sizeable group of people

When we read about the patriarchs in the Old Testament, it is
important to remember that they did not have a New Testament. That
sounds very obvious. Yet it is amazing how many Christians appear
to forget this in the judgements they make about them, for example
condemning Abraham for adultery over the child he fathered with his
wife's Egyptian slave girl, Hagar. No, the custom of the time allowed a
childless couple to use a slave as a substitute wife to produce a child for
them. Neither did the Patriarchs even have any Old Testament since
they stand at its opening. What they did have was a personal relationship
with God.

This was expressed on their part through faith and prayer and the
building of altars on which to offer sacrifices. The function of the latter

was not yet clearly defined. As yet they had no priesthood, no religious festivals and apparently no official centre for worship.

⋘

Abraham may be dated about four thousand years ago, that is around 2000 BC. The patriarchs lived as long before the time of Christ as the time of Christ is removed from us. To grasp what is written about them we must try to understand the culture in which they lived, a culture so very different from our own.

The patriarchs were semi-nomads. A nomad is a person who lives in a tent and travels around with his flocks and herds, seeking pasture and water for them. But he would not travel alone, but in a family or clan group. So how can a person be a semi-nomad, half a nomad? Genesis 26:12 gives us the clue to that. Sometimes these people stayed in a suitable area long enough to grow some crops. So they were partly dependent on their animals and partly on their crops; part nomad, part farmer.

The picture is one of a time when Canaan, roughly the area of modern Israel plus the Palestinian territories, was sparsely settled by its different tribes of local inhabitants. But there was space for nomadic peoples to come and go.

⋘

So it was around 2000 BC that God spoke to Abraham promising to give to him and his descendants the land of Canaan. It was His intention that all peoples of the earth would be blessed through Abraham's descendants. This promise was made when Abraham was both childless and landless. Abraham came from a culture where other gods were worshipped, but the Lord called him. As always the initiative lay with God.

Why call a man in this way?

14

God was setting in motion His rescue plan for humanity. He would prepare a people amongst whom He Himself would come to live as man. So there was the need for one group of people to be prepared for this. One group was chosen, so that in the end all races could be blessed. How would all peoples of the earth be blessed through Abraham? When Jesus came among Abraham's descendants and as one of them, then the good news of God's gracious deliverance from sin and its consequences became available for all people.

∽

You will enjoy the story of Abraham. Yes, he rose on occasions to great heights of faith. You may have heard about those bits in church. What you probably won't have heard about was that he had some crashing defeats as well, besides several occasions when he got on the wrong track simply by taking things into his own hands and deciding he could work them out himself. So his story turns out to be very much like ours and one from which we can learn a great deal.

First of all he makes a promising start. He does obey God in going to Canaan, though when he set out, God had not actually told him where He was leading him. But then, when there was a famine in Canaan, he nipped off down to Egypt and earned himself a well deserved rebuke from the Pharaoh himself! Yet he was generous to his somewhat hapless nephew Lot. When the latter got captured by some raiders, Abraham carried out a lightning military campaign to rescue him from his captors.

God made a covenant with Abraham promising Canaan to him and his descendants of whom there were still none. The sign of this covenant was that his male descendants were to be circumcised on the eighth day after their birth.. Circumcision was an accepted puberty rite amongst most of the surrounding tribes, but here it was given a totally different timing and significance for Abraham and his descendants.

Since Abraham was old and the promised son showed no sign of coming from his wife Sarah, he tried following local custom and using her slave girl, Hagar as a substitute wife. So Ishmael was born. It was some fourteen years later that Abraham and Sarah had the promised son, Isaac.

This covenant promise made by God to Abraham passes down to Isaac and then to Jacob his son. Isaac appears as a comparatively colourless figure, but he was an essential link in the chain, perhaps some comfort to all of us who may feel we have not made a great mark on human history!

Jacob starts off by driving a hard bargain with his brother Esau to obtain his birthright, the right of inheritance of the older son. Then, when Isaac thinks he is dying and wants to bless his elder son Esau, Jacob, who is egged on by his mother, Rebekah, comes to his father pretending to be Esau. As Isaac's sight is failing, Jacob is not recognised and so he steals the blessing. To escape from Esau's murderous wrath, Jacob then flees the country and goes to his mother's brother, Laban.

Tangling with Uncle Laban gave Jacob a taste of his own medicine. First go he was married to the cousin he didn't want, before he could have the one he loved. Yet he went to Laban alone and with nothing and twenty years later returned to Canaan with two wives, two slave girls, eleven sons, one daughter and considerable herds of livestock. He was grateful for the way in which God had been with him and had looked after him.

But you will say, "Jacob had twelve sons". Yes, but the twelfth, Benjamin, was born after he returned to Canaan.

Jacob faced up to the unavoidable meeting with Esau and then put as much distance between the two of them as he could. He continued to live in Canaan, and proved quite unable to control his sons.

Yet Jacob, Isaac's son, twister and deceiver that he was, took hold of the promises of God and made them his own. He knew that God had helped and protected him throughout his life. For many for whom life is a rough struggle there is much help and comfort to be had from reading and reflecting on Jacob's story.

∽

But by now there is tension between the promise given to Abraham and his descendants and its fulfilment. There were the descendants now, but they owned no land beyond a burial site which Abraham had purchased from the local inhabitants when Sarah died.

Yes, Jacob, whose other name was now Israel, was well off for descendants. So his descendants are the sons of Israel. Thus they are the Israelites of the Old Testament. No they were not Jews. Neither were they Israelis. Jews are descended from the later Southern Kingdom of Judah. The people of God in most of the Old Testament are the Israelites. (The Jews are Israelites anyway!)

Let's try and sort this one out. Do you see that the twelve sons of Jacob/Israel give rise to the Israelites. Now one of Jacob's sons was Judah. When the Israelite kingdom divided into two after the death of Solomon, the smaller southern kingdom, which actually contained the tribe of Simeon as well as Judah, was named Judah. It is these people who began to be called Jews after the seventh century or thereabouts,. But they could also properly be called Israelites, for they also were descended from Jacob whose other name was Israel. So all Jews are also Israelites. But in Old Testament times, not all Israelites were Jews, only those from the Southern Kingdom, Judah. Admittedly by New Testament times the term appears to cover anyone of Israelite descent. (Israelis don't come into it until the establishment of modern Israel in the middle of the last century.)

There had been periodic famine in Canaan in the times of both Abraham and Isaac. But now there was a much more severe and widespread famine which could have threatened Jacob and his whole extended family with starvation.

But God had been preparing for that well in advance of its occurrence. Jacob's ten older sons had sold number eleven, Joseph, and he ended up as top slave in an Egyptian household. Read Genesis 37 carefully and you will understand why the brothers did it. Perhaps if you had a brother like Joseph was then, you might have thought of selling him! Not that the brothers' evil plan was at God's prompting or desire, but He did show how He could turn a potentially horrible situation round and make it a blessing to all concerned. That just needed the co-operation of the main character involved, namely Joseph.

Joseph's thirteen years, first as slave, albeit one with considerable responsibilities, and then as prisoner, were the training for the prominent position he was to occupy. He had opportunity to learn the Egyptian language, to acquire and display the administrative and personnel management skills he would later need. He had to learn to get along with all kinds of people. It is likely that those in an Egyptian prison would not be the easiest companions!

While Joseph was in  prison he interpreted the dreams of two of the Pharaoh's officers who were imprisoned with him. One of these was subsequently released and re-instated and promptly forgot all about Joseph until Pharaoh himself had dreams that troubled him. Then at his prompting, Joseph was called out of prison and summoned before Pharaoh and he interpreted these dreams too, though he was careful to tell Pharaoh that it was God who enabled him to do this.

The interpretation of these dreams alerted Pharaoh to the seven year famine which was to come on the land after seven years of bumper crops.

Joseph also outlined a scheme to deal with the situation. As a result of this, Joseph was placed in charge of food storage and distribution in Egypt. So later on he was able to provide for his whole family who would otherwise have come to ruin.

Joseph was also given an Egyptian wife and they had his two sons, Manasseh and Ephraim. In those times names each had a meaning. These names show that Joseph had put the painful past well behind him and that he was grateful to God for the way He had made him fruitful in Egypt. He was well aware of the grave wrong his brothers had done him, but he did not hold it against them, for he saw how God had worked his life out for good.

So eventually Joseph's brothers came to buy corn in Egypt. At first they had no idea that the man with whom they were dealing was Joseph, though he recognised them at once. They never imagined that their dastardly act of selling him as a slave would lead to his becoming the equivalent of Prime Minister of Egypt, whereas he knew that sooner or later they would either have to come to buy food from him or starve.

Twenty-two years earlier the brothers had no scruples about selling Joseph and telling their father, Jacob, that he had been torn by wild beasts. Before he can send them back to Jacob to bring the whole family down to Canaan, Joseph must devise some plan to find out whether they have changed. Could they now be trusted to go home to Jacob, admit to him what they had done to Joseph and then bring their father and the whole family down to Egypt? This is what lies behind Joseph's imprisonment of Simeon and his later threat to detain Benjamin.

This leads to Judah in particular showing his true colours. Yes, he has changed. Years earlier Judah had initiated the sale of Joseph and was quite ready to let Jacob believe he had been killed by some wild beast. But now he was willing to remain in Egypt as a slave, if only Benjamin can return safely to his father, Jacob. Joseph assures his brothers of the forgiveness he had had for them years earlier. He tries to get them to see God's purpose in all that had happened to him and the way God had worked his life out to save them, along with many other people, from starvation.

# Israel in Egypt: Exodus 1-2

SO THE ENTIRE FAMILY OF Jacob, whose other name was Israel, moved to Egypt. The whole scene has changed. Not only are the descendants of Abraham now living in Egypt, but they increase greatly in numbers. They probably would have been very content to mind their own business, but as often happens when there is a fast increasing minority of people of another race, the original and dominant people become suspicious. This still happens today as we know all too well.

Way after Joseph's time the new Pharaoh of Egypt was unaware of the benefit Joseph's administration had brought to his whole country . He was now afraid that if war broke out the Israelites would join Egypt's enemies and leave the country. The Egyptians were soon using the Israelites as their labour force on various building projects and though they would find it difficult to do without them, yet because of their groundless fears, they tried to get rid of them.

So the Pharaoh tried a couple of times to initiate a policy which would exterminate the Israelite new-born boys. First their mid-wives were ordered to kill them at birth and, when it was quite clear that they would not do this, then new-born boys were to be thrown into the Nile. Get rid of the boys and the girls would end up as extra wives or slaves of the Egyptians and the whole Israelite race would disappear in generation or two.

One boy, Moses, was placed in the Nile in a waterproof basket and was rescued by one of Pharaoh's daughters. (Remember that the Pharaoh would have a large harem and probably had enough bother to count his offspring, let alone know what they were doing!) The child's sister, Miriam, who had been lurking nearby to see what happened, offered to find a wet nurse for the baby and, of course, chose her own mother. So Pharaoh's daughter paid Moses' mother to look after him until after he was weaned. Weaning would not take place until a child was three to five years old and the text of Exodus implies that Moses may have stayed with his mother for longer than this before being handed over to Pharaoh's daughter again. So much for the Pharaoh's edict! A Hebrew child was brought up and educated as if he was the son of Pharaoh's daughter!

When he was forty years old or so Moses fled from Egypt into the Sinai desert. He had become so angry at the way the Israelites were being treated that he killed one of the Egyptian foremen whom he saw beating an Israelite. When he realised that this had become known and that the Pharaoh was prepared to have him killed, he had no option but to leave Egypt and go out into the Sinai desert. Here he met up with Jethro, the father of some shepherdesses and stayed with him, where he helped look after his flocks and married one of his daughters.

Meanwhile the Egyptians continued to use the Israelites as slave labour for building two store cities, Pithom and Rameses.. Things got worse and worse for them and they became increasingly distressed. But God knew about their hardships. He would act on their behalf because He would be faithful to His covenant with Abraham.

God knows what He is doing. He did then and He does now.

For Moses, the man who must later lead Israel, was nursed by his own mother so he could know who he really was. During his early years he lived in his own family and so he could learn about his people and His God.

Moses, the man who must confront Pharaoh, was then educated in Pharaoh's palace and so he knew all the requirements of Egyptian customs.

Moses, the man who must lead Israel through the Sinai peninsular, spent 40 years shepherding in that same wilderness so he would know its paths, its oases, its weather like the back of his hand. You can't get a tailor-made training course to match that at any of our modern colleges, now can you? Even if you could, the fact that it took eighty years is something many might find a bit of a drawback in these hurried days! God is never in a hurry.

# *Deliverance from Egyptian Oppression: Exodus 3-18.*

WHEN GOD TOLD MOSES HE was the one who would lead the Israelites out of Egypt, it was a very different Moses from the man who had killed the Egyptian overseer forty years earlier. Then he had been prepared to be a self appointed deliverer for the Israelites. Now he was very reluctant to accept God's call, coming up with one excuse after another.

And when Moses did confront Pharaoh with God's command to release the Israelites Pharaoh first responded with harsher oppression. To be fair God had taken care to warn Moses that Pharaoh would only let the Israelites go if He compelled him to do so.

First God used His own creation to send nine warning plagues on Egypt. The waters of the River Nile turned to blood, the land was overrun with frogs first of all, then gnats, and then flies. There was a plague on livestock, then boils on both people and livestock. Then there was a most destructive hailstorm. After that locusts arrived to eat any greenery that was left and then there was darkness for three days. Some of these plagues were definitely one in the eye for the Egyptian gods, for example both the Nile and the sun were worshipped there.

These plagues gained in intensity and destructiveness as they went on. At first both Egyptians and Israelites suffered from them, but with the later ones, the Israelites were not affected. Warnings were given before the plagues, so that those who took note of these could protect themselves to some extent. These early plagues did not necessarily involve loss of life. But the Pharaoh, against the opinion of some of his advisers, was adamant that he would not let the Israelites go. Having refused the warnings, he would now have to face the judgement which could have been averted.

So God passes through Egypt in judgement. Remember that the Pharaoh had ordered the death of all new-born Israelite boys. God had said that Israel was His firstborn son. There is a principle in the OT that the punishment fits the crime.

God would pass through the land of Egypt and the firstborn in each Egyptian household would die. But where a lamb had been sacrificed it would be different. Its blood was to be placed on doorpost and lintels. (No, God didn't need it to know which households were Israelite! He was already aware of that.) But this action showed that the residents had acted on God's word. They had taken what He said seriously. Thus they had expressed their faith in Him. Faith takes God at His word and acts on it.

So when God passed through Egypt in judgement, the firstborn of the Egyptians would die. But He would pass over these Israelite households and they would be safe. So you see why the Israelites celebrated this as the Pass-over.

On the night of the Passover Pharaoh had had enough. He expelled the Israelites from Egypt that there and then.

Very soon after expelling the Israelites from Egypt, Pharaoh changed his mind and sent his army after them. He could not afford to let such a valuable labour force go like that! The Israelites' situation did look desperate as they were hemmed in by impassable water in front of them and the Egyptian army behind. The water was the Red Sea of Bible translations. Actually, as a footnote in your Bible will tell you, it was the Sea of Reeds. Precisely where it was no-one is totally sure: remember that geography can change quite a bit over a period of more than three thousand years. The point is that the Israelites were completely stuck, with water in front of them and the Egyptian army behind. Their situation was hopeless....apparently.

But God protected the Israelites overnight and then He caused a strong East wind to blow so that the waters were parted and Israel was able to walk through on dry land. So again the Creator is using His creation for His purposes.

Ill-advisedly the Egyptians with their chariots decided to pursue the Israelites and so their chariot wheels were caught by the softer ground and the returning waters. Thus the Israelites were free and they knew they owed that freedom to God's power. But they were unaccustomed to freedom and had much to learn through the immediate hardships of their journey.

This could have been around 1280 BC. Some go for date up to a couple of hundred years before this and they could well be right. But to opt for one possible date is better than leaving this vital event floating free in time. The Old Testament happened in history, it all took place in this world of ours.

Through the Passover, the Exodus and the crossing of the Red Sea God had done for Israel what she knew she could never do for herself. God had delivered her, rescued her, redeemed her, saved her. In both testaments God is consistently the God who rescues His people out of His compassion for them. Remember salvation is rescue, deliverance.

It is important to grasp the enormous significance of these events: Passover, Exodus and the crossing of the Red Sea in the Old Testament. Do you see that it is through these events that God reveals Himself as the Saviour and Redeemer of His people? From now on the Israelites are the redeemed people of God. So the Law is given, not that they might get Brownie points and climb up to God's standard, but to show how a redeemed people should live out their gratitude to their God. It is the failure to understand the significance of these events which skews so many people's understanding of the Old Testament.

These events, Passover, Exodus and the crossing of the Red Sea, are as vital and critically important to the Old Testament story as the Cross and Resurrection of Christ are to the New Testament. Did you know that the Old Testament looks back to Passover, Exodus and the crossing of the Red Sea over 150 times? Keep a look out for the way in which these references are used when you come across them in your reading of the Old Testament. So all this emphasises the importance of these events for overall understanding of the Old Testament. This is not just one story amongst many: it is the pivotal point of the Old Testament and immensely important for grasping that God is the same God of grace and salvation throughout the whole Bible.

✺

The one thing the Israelites had been sure of in slavery in Egypt was a good food supply. That was not so readily available in the Sinai desert and this led to grumbling in a very short time. However, God provided food for the Israelites on a daily basis during their trek to Canaan. So they began to learn to be dependent on Him as they could collect this food only on the day it was needed.

# The Sinai Covenant:
# Exodus 19-24, 32-33

So God had rescued His people from Egypt. He had delivered them from slavery. All the initiative had come from God. But how was Israel's new relationship with God to be maintained?

You have no doubt heard about the Ten Commandments, even if you cannot recite them in order, (or out of order)! You probably know that God gave these commands to Israel after she had come out of Egypt. What you were unlikely to have been told was that these commands were not a thing in themselves, but were the core principles of the Sinai Covenant which God made with Israel.

The preparations for this covenant emphasised the holiness of God. 'Holy' is a much misused and misunderstood word. No, it is not just another word for good, pure or upright. When it applies to God it emphasises the distinctiveness of God from all else, His otherness compared with everything else we know. 'Holy' as applied to God refers to His being separate, distinct, different. Then, because of His character, 'holy' took on a secondary meaning of moral purity.

But we need to note the fundamental difference between a holy God and a holy people. God's holiness is part of His essential character. You can't have God without His holiness. But for His people their holiness is derived from their relationship with Him.

So as far as Israel was concerned 'holy' meant primarily 'devoted to God, set aside for His exclusive use.' In this sense objects or buildings also could be holy when they were set aside for God's use only.

❧

The Covenant at Sinai was not just a contract or agreement. It was more like the sort of vassal treaty which was often made in the Ancient Near East in those times. The overlord or great king makes all the conditions and the vassal, the subject nation or tribe agrees to them. One does not negotiate with God! So it is covenant in something of a 'last will and testament' sense. You can accept the terms and receive the benefits, but you cannot alter it for your convenience. So this explains why the first section of your Bible is called the Old Testament. It is the Old Covenant. You will remember that earlier on God had made a covenant with Noah and then a covenant with Abraham, but it is more this Sinai Covenant which leads to part of our Bible being called the Old Testament.

The value of a covenant relationship is you know where you stand. Israel under the old covenant knew where she stood with God. Under the New Covenant, established by the death of Jesus Christ, Christians too know where they stand with God.

In this covenant at Sinai, God gives the Law to Israel. That is much more than the Ten Commandments. In fact, you will find the covenant law in various places between Exodus 20 and the end of Deuteronomy. If you think that is a lot, ask any solicitor you know how many feet of bookshelf English law would take! Israel's part was to obey God's law in order to show her gratitude to Him..

The commandments were not a ladder to get to God, but showed an already redeemed people how to live as God's people. The Ten Commandments were given to Israel, not to mankind in general. Remember God never operated a system of Brownie points, not even in the Old Testament. The Law was given to Israel because she was already God's nation. She can express her gratitude to God, and her consciousness of being His, by obedience to these laws. In much the same way Jesus says in John Chapter 14 that those who love Him obey Him, while those who do not obey His commandments do not love Him. In both testaments it's as simple as that.

❧

My Ulster Protestant student had found her way through the laws in this part of Old Testament.. To her surprise it all made sense. She wrote, "This says that what matters is our relationship with God and our behaviour towards other people." Her summary of the law is excellent.

❧

At the beginning of Exodus 20, the Ten Commandments' chapter, God reminded Israel that He had redeemed her . That fact was the basis for the giving of the Law, it was the foundation for the establishment of the covenant.

First and foremost God required His people's exclusive loyalty and obedience: Very literally 'You shall have no other gods before My Face,' that is, 'in My Presence'. That does not leave anywhere much to have other gods! To worship anything other than God would be to worship something far less than God, something man-made, either a figment of man's mind or the work of his hands.

Rewards of blessing for obedience to the covenant were set down and so were curses, punishments for disobedience. It does make sense that you can only have the benefits of any particular relationship while you are loyal to that relationship. For example a wayward son may be truly loved by both parents, but he can only enjoy and benefit from that love if he chooses to remain in a good relationship with them. If he runs off and ignores his parents, then he may still be loved, but he will not experience the good of that love. So if Israel chose to turn her back on the Lord by worshipping other gods, she forfeited the benefits that He wanted her to have. But because God is loving and compassionate, He did not give up on her in spite of her habitual waywardness.

It was only a matter of weeks after Israel had come out of Egypt that she fell into idolatry, thus breaking the newly established covenant. Aaron, Moses' brother, who really should have known better, made a golden calf and then the Israelites worshipped it with some very dubious rites. Aaron said it was the god who had brought all them out of Egypt. Later when questioned rather closely by Moses, Aaron said that he threw the gold into the fire and this calf came out! Somehow Moses was not convinced that it had all happened quite like that.

So as Moses came down Mount Sinai, God had alerted him to what had happened in the Israelite camp and Moses smashed the two copies of the commandments. Moses' action in breaking the stone tablets on which the covenant was written simply ratified the fact that the covenant had been broken. There were normally two copies of a covenant, one would be kept in the temple of the god of each of the two parties to the covenant. In Israel's case, both copies of the Ten Commandments, the core of the covenant, were to be housed in the Ark of the Covenant, a fact which explains its name.

᪥

If the God of the Old Testament was anything like most people imagine, then surely He would have finished with Israel, or finished off Israel completely, there and then and that would have been the end of the story. But it is not. He did punish the Israelites, but He persevered with them. There are various suggested meanings of the Hebrew name Israel, but one of them is 'God perseveres'. He did with them and He does with us!

# Israel's System of Worship: Exodus 25-40

MUCH OF THE LAST FIFTEEN chapters of the book of Exodus is taken up with the instructions for building a portable place of worship, the tabernacle, and making everything needed for this. There are also full instructions for making the garments for the high priest. Then we read of these tasks being accomplished.

This all might sound less exciting than the first twenty or so chapters of the book, but it is of great importance. God's purpose was to dwell among His people. He was not just setting them free to go off and do their own thing: anyway freedom is never found that way. The most free person on this earth is the one who most fulfils the will of God and so lives in His Presence. God is indeed holy, that is distinct, different and separate from all that there is, but He is by no means indifferent to anything He has made. He wanted to live amongst His people, close to them, available to them and all this tabernacle building and so forth was His way of making that possible.

The tabernacle or tent had an outer courtyard, containing the altar for burnt offerings. Nearer the tabernacle itself stood the laver (wash bowl) for ritual cleansing of the priests. The 'walls' of the actual tabernacle were made of wooden boards overlaid with gold. Great curtains formed the roof and covered the sides, the inner curtain being of blue, purple and scarlet cloth.

The actual tent itself had two parts. The first, the Holy Place, could only be entered by priests on duty. The second, the Holy of Holies, or Most Holy Place, could only be entered by the high priest himself on the Day of Atonement. This was because it was thought to be the very presence of God Himself. So the tabernacle was made because God would live and move amongst His people. When the glory of the Lord filled the tabernacle right at the end of Exodus, then we have the real climax of this story. This is the goal of all those instructions about tabernacle and priestly garments and such like. God was present amongst His people.

See the way in which the approach to the tabernacle and its different parts emphasise the holiness of God. Passing through the entrance and into the tabernacle courtyard, the first piece of tabernacle furniture which one would see was the altar of burnt offering. Here sacrifices for the removal of sin were offered. Then there was the priests' laver/wash bowl near the entrance to the Tabernacle itself. So the priest on duty had to undergo a ritual cleansing. Only the priests on duty could go into the Holy Place. Only the High Priest himself could go into the Holy of Holies once a year, taking with him the blood of a sacrificial animal.

# More on Israel's System of Worship: Leviticus

Amongst other things the setting up of the Sinai Covenant had revealed God's holiness. The Golden Calf incident only a few weeks after that had emphasised human sinfulness and fickleness, rebelliousness and disobedience, in spite of all that God had done for His people. So how could a relationship between the holy God and these sinful humans be maintained? How could this relationship be repaired when it was damaged through human disobedience?

This is where the book of Leviticus comes in. There is a great need to understand the purpose for which Leviticus was written. Yes, with no refrigeration in a hot country, it might be good hygiene advice not to eat pork. With no medical care, it might be good to isolate those with suspicious skin conditions.

But this is not what Leviticus is about. I want to say that as loudly as I possibly can! Leviticus is about holiness not hygiene! All these regulations are there because God, who is holy, dwelt with His people. How could the Israelite camp be fit for a holy God?

Here we need to understand some categories which don't usually come into our thinking nowadays. Persons and objects could be in one of three states.

They could be holy, dedicated to God.

Or they could be clean, normal, pure in which case they could be used in the service of God.

But if they were in the third category of unclean that is abnormal, impure, sinful, defiled, mixed, confused, then it was dangerous for them to be brought near God. for the holy and the unclean must never mix.

(Clean and unclean here have no real relation to our ideas of washed and unwashed, clean and dirty.)

So what was to happen when Israel infringed God's law and so became unclean or defiled? How could the relationship between man and God be restored?

This is where the sacrificial system comes in. Instructions for the different sacrifices are given in the first seven chapters of Leviticus These sacrifices were the whole burnt offering, the grain offering, the fellowship offering, the sin offering and the guilt offering. Remember Israel was a people who could rarely afford to eat meat. Wealth had horns and hooves. So these sacrifices were costly. Notice how some of them were graded as to what people could afford, or on the basis of the position in the community of the offerer.

The one who had broken God's law could bring an unblemished animal. He would identify with it, pressing his hands on its head. He would slaughter it, and then he would prepare it for the altar where it would be burned by the priest. To approach a holy God is a serious and costly business.

With some offerings certain sections of the animal were assigned to the priests as their share. The fellowship offering was largely eaten by the worshipper and his family in the presence of God.

The sacrificial system also prepared for the One Great Sacrifice which was to come. Without this OT preparation we would have no way of interpreting, and thus fully benefiting from, the sacrifice of Jesus Christ on the cross. Think about that

❧

The sacrificial system needed people to administer it. Aaron, Moses' brother, is appointed as high priest and his four sons as priests.

It is too little recognised that a high point spiritually can also be a point of maximum danger. No sooner had Aaron and his sons been invested with the priesthood than two of his sons decided that it was all right to do their own thing and offer to God what fire they fancied. This deliberate disobedience cost them their lives and the Israelites were beginning to learn that a Holy God is not to be trifled with.

We also come across lists of clean and unclean foods and certain conditions which render persons unclean, in most cases temporarily, with rites for their cleansing being outlined. All this might seem far removed from us, but it can serve to help us remember that belonging to a holy God touches absolutely every aspect of our lives. For the Israelites these regulations were a continual reminder that since their God was holy, they too were to be holy in every aspect of their lives. How much we Christians need such a reminder today.

❧

Of the various annual religious festivals established for the Israelites, the Day of Atonement receives the fullest treatment. The other festivals we find in Leviticus are Passover, commemorating the rescue of Israel from Egypt closely followed closely by Unleavened Bread. Then seven weeks later there is the Feast of Weeks (or Pentecost) giving thanks for the grain harvest. The giving of the Law at Sinai was also celebrated on this occasion..

In the seventh month, which would be our September/October there was first of all, the Feast of Trumpets announcing the civil New Year. This was followed by the Day of Atonement, when even the tabernacle itself must be cleansed from the defilement incurred by its use throughout the previous year. (Remember this cleansing was not a spring-clean, but the application of sacrificial blood by the high priest.) On this occasion cleansing rituals were performed not only for the Tabernacle but also for the high priest and the Israelites themselves.

Finally the Feast of Tabernacles celebrated the grape harvest and the end of the agricultural season. So these last three all took place in the seventh month and because the Israelite calendar differed from ours this would be September or October. That sounds a bit vague, but the Israelites followed a lunar calendar and so had to have a leap year every two or three years. But they had to insert, not one extra day, but a whole month. As you know, we follow a solar calendar and so the insertion of one extra day every four years keeps our calendars correct. The Israelites' festivals always occurred on the same dates in their calendar, but these would not be the same dates in ours.

There are several chapters more of covenant law in Leviticus. Laws both here and in Deuteronomy strongly forbid any kind of occult practices. These, of whatever kind they may be, are all an attempt to control the supernatural as an aid to getting one's own way. By contrast faith in God is concerned with obedience to Him and so getting His will done.

᪗

Did you know that the commandment, "Love your neighbour as yourself" makes its first Bible appearance there in Leviticus 19:18?

Near its conclusion Leviticus has a chapter outlining the blessings Israel would experience if she remained within the covenant and walked with her God and the curses she would experience if she chose to disobey Him, abandon His covenant and follow other gods.

Yet, though there would be the punishment of exile for Israel if she abandoned the covenant, there was also the promise that God would remember His covenant and however much it had been broken and repudiated by Israel, He would still be faithful. So because of the character of God, there could be no situation without hope.

Keep this in mind as you read on and find out what really did happen and which path Israel chose for herself.

# *Grumbles and Rebellion Numbers.*

ON TO THE BOOK OF Numbers. This, among other things, is the story of the grumblers. Here lists and censuses and laws alternate with narrative as the Israelites progress on their journey from Egypt to Canaan.

From Israel the tribe of Levi had been selected to carry out all the duties to do with the tabernacle. It was clearly set out precisely how the tabernacle was to be handled to take it apart and move it from place to place. Perhaps one should point out that some parts of it, like the Ark of the Covenant, were never to be actually touched. Such parts had been fitted out with long carrying poles which ensured that those who removed them could do so without ever touching them. (That is why God acts in judgement when these regulations were flouted! 2 Samuel 6.) A solemn ceremony then took place in which the Levites were purified in preparation for their task.

With all that God had done for the Israelites, rescuing them from slavery in Egypt, feeding them day by day and offering them a way of keeping in fellowship with Himself, one might expect a spark of gratitude from the recipients. Not a bit of it. Granted moving across the

Sinai desert was not that much easier than life in Egypt had been. But had Israel obeyed God that journey need not have taken very long.

First of all the Israelites grumbled about the hardships of their journey. Next they grumbled about the food God provided for them day by day. It was, they said, not a patch on the cucumbers, melons, leeks, garlic and onions they enjoyed in Egypt. They complained constantly and that is the best possible way to feel miserable. Lots of people in our current society are proving that! I expect you know some of them.

Next even Moses' brother, Aaron, and sister, Miriam, began talking against him.

Much more serious trouble came when Moses sent out one leader from each of the twelve tribes of Israel to have a good look round Canaan with a view to its conquest.

Ten came back with their eyes on themselves and so magnified the problems involved in the conquest of the land that they said it couldn't be done. Only two of the leaders, Joshua and Caleb took God into account and said that He could enable them to conquer it.

But the Israelites joined the ten in their unbelief and brought judgement on that whole generation. This judgement was that instead of going ahead to conquer Canaan right away, they would now spend forty years in the wilderness, till that unbelieving generation had died out.

Even that did not stop the rebellions. A Levite named Korah and two other men, Dathan and Abiram, challenged Moses' leadership along with the support of another 250 leaders from amongst the Israelites. Later when the people arrived at a place with no water they blamed Moses for this. On yet another occasion they spoke against God and against Moses. Yes, God did punish them for these things, but He did not give up on them. He persevered with them in spite of everything. Would you have felt like persevering with them after all this?

✎

When at last Israel was getting near Canaan the little kingdom of Moab felt itself to be threatened. So Balak, king of Moab, called a heathen prophet named Baalam to curse Israel for him. God overruled and to Balak's disgust, Balaam blessed Israel instead. That probably displeased Balaam as much as Balak, because now he would not get the rich reward with which Balak had tempted him. But Balaam found a deadlier weapon against Israel. He stirred up the Moabites to lead Israel into idolatry by worshipping the Baal of Peor with rites which would have been thoroughly objectionable to God. (Numbers 25, 31:15-16, Revelation 2:14)

◈

The Israelites were divided into twelve tribes, each taking both their name and their descent from one of the twelve sons of Jacob. Well that is the theory! But instead of one tribe of Joseph, there are two, named not after Joseph, but after his two sons, Ephraim and Manasseh. (Genesis 48:5) Even with modern arithmetic skills it should be apparent that this gives a total of thirteen tribes. Twelve would have an inheritance, that is an area of the land where they could settle, when they got to Canaan, while the tribe of Levi, whose function was to see to the tabernacle and later the temple, would live in 48 cities scattered throughout the other tribal holdings. They would have pasture land allocated to them for their livestock. But they would not have a tribal inheritance, an area of land assigned to their tribe, like the other tribes had.

Here at the end of Numbers two and a half tribes, Reuben, Gad and half of Manasseh chose to settle east of the Jordan in land conquered by the Israelites on the last stage of their journey to Canaan. Notice how touchy relationships between the tribes are at this point when you read about this settlement.

# God loves His People: Deuteronomy

In Deuteronomy Moses reminds Israel of the way God had rescued her from Egypt and then led her through the wilderness. He further explains the covenant God had made with Israel.

God had not chosen Israel because of anything special or appealing about her. She was a small and insignificant group of people. He had chosen her because He loved her and now He bound her to exclusive loyalty to Himself A suitable response from Israel would be for her to love, serve, fear and obey God and to cling to Him. In the Old Testament faith in God is never seen as just a religion. It is something which affects, directs and instructs the totality of life. The same must be said of anything which can rightly be described as Christianity.

The laws found in Deuteronomy, showing how Israel should live as God's people, are mostly similar to ones already found in Exodus to Numbers.

Finally Deuteronomy closes with outlining the blessings Israel would experience if she were obedient to the covenant and the curses which would befall her if she chose to disregard it. It is set before her as a choice between life and death, with an impassioned plea that she should choose life.

So we are at the end of the first five books of the Old Testament, variously called the Law, the Law of Moses or the Pentateuch. Pentateuch means five scrolls since originally each of the five books would take up a whole scroll. Law from the Hebrew word 'Torah' is a much wider word than our English word 'law'. It speaks of the whole will and purpose of God.

So after all, Abraham had had descendants a-plenty. But beyond a burial site, he had owned no land. That part of the promise was about to find its fulfilment.

# The Conquest of Canaan: Joshua

THE THEME OF THE BOOK of Joshua is God's faithful fulfilment of His promises. Israel is at last to occupy Canaan, the land promised to Abraham. Since the death of Moses is recorded at the end of Deuteronomy, Joshua, who had been with him as an apprentice for a long time, was now appointed to lead the Israelites into Canaan.

Remember Canaan was a country about the size of Wales and somewhat more mountainous. It was organised in a system of city states. If we had that same system where I live now, then in and around Herefordshire we would have the King of Ross-on-Wye, the King of Ledbury, the King of Leominster, and yes not far away, the King of Hay-on-Wye. So that is why Joshua can defeat 31 kings in such a comparatively small area.

Israel is commanded to destroy the Canaanites, to carry out the sacred ban, to effect total destruction. There are several points to bear in mind here, though they may not wholly alleviate all the problems you might feel with this.

Way back in Genesis 15:16 God had told Abraham that He will not let him have Canaan for several hundred more years as the sin of the Amorite (more or less equivalent to Canaanite here) has not yet reached its full measure. In other words God was giving the Amorites/Canaanites ample opportunity to change their ways. They had an extra few hundred years in which to repent! But they had continued their disgusting worship of the Baals which involved sexual fertility rites and child sacrifice and which contaminated the rest of their moral scene also. (See Deuteronomy 18:9-13 for an account of some of the things they were doing) A holy God will not tolerate this sort of thing for ever. So they are now placed under the sacred ban, which means they are to be destroyed. Deuteronomy 9:4-6 is another of several passages which speaks of the wickedness of the peoples whom the Israelites were to drive out of Canaan.

We skew our understanding of what happened if we try to apply modern terms like genocide or ethnic cleansing to what took place here. The issue was not race, but religious practices and moral corruption. There comes a time when a just God will judge evil. The Old Testament sees Israel's conquest of Canaan as that judgement.

Joshua's conquest of Canaan was a three pronged campaign.

First of all the Israelites arrived somewhere near the centre of country. I guess you know how they captured Jericho. (You will find it interesting to notice how many Old Testament battles the Israelites win without fighting.) The battle for nearby Ai was a different matter where the Israelites' disobedience found them out. By this time news of their progress was spreading through Canaan and a group of towns, headed by Gibeon, joined together and succeeded in duping the Israelites into making a covenant with them to protect them. When the Gibeonite ruse was uncovered, the Israelites felt bound to remain loyal to this agreement.

Then Joshua dealt with the South including Jerusalem and its allies before turning his attention to the north, where the main opposition was led by King Jabin of Hazor.

The second half of the book of Joshua notes the incompleteness of the conquest as the land is divided between twelve tribes. The Canaanites still held the plains. Some cities reported as conquered in the first half of Joshua later reappear in Canaanite hands. That is hardly surprising. If the Canaanites were defeated at a certain location and it was not then adequately occupied, there was nothing to stop them taking it over again. In some cases that is likely to be what happened.

Finally Joshua challenges Israel to wholehearted obedience to God in response to His faithfulness. Yes, of course the Israelites say "We will serve the Lord our God and obey Him."

As we move on into the book of Judges and beyond we will see what they actually did, which sadly was something quite different from what they had just promised.

# An Odd Assortment of Deliverers: Judges

WHAT DO YOU EXPECT TO find in a book headed 'Judges'? Probably not what you will find here! These judges are not chaps with long curled grey wigs. Neither do they listen carefully and sift evidence: they are not the type for that sort of thing. (I don't think Abimelech of Judges 10 would know what evidence was, let alone listen to it!)

Here the word 'judge' is not used in the sense of someone who has to help decide on innocence or guilt and, in the latter case, set a penalty. No, this sort of judge is someone who vindicates you, who stands up for your rights, who delivers you. He could almost be called a saviour. (It is in this sense that we often find the psalmist praying, 'Lord, judge me!' which may otherwise sound odd to our English ears!)

The book of Judges opens with different tribal groups in Israel seeking the Lord's advice about taking or re-taking some of the territory of Canaan. We learn how several of the tribes had been unable to take over their allotted tribal territories, but instead were living alongside the native Canaanite inhabitants. Very soon they were intermarrying with them and worshipping their gods. So we don't get far in the book before we are introduced to a pattern which was to be repeated several times.

It is this. First Israel broke the Sinai covenant by worshipping the local Canaanite gods.

Then the Israelites were oppressed by one of the neighbouring tribes.

After a bit they came to their senses and cried to the Lord for help against their oppressors.

Then He raised up for them a judge who delivered them from their oppressor. The Israelites then behaved themselves for the remaining lifetime of that judge, but relapsed into idolatry again after his death.... and so on!

How long all this took is a matter of some discussion. The answer depends partly on whether the Exodus was as late as the date suggested earlier on and partly on whether some of the judges could have been contemporary with one another, as some of them appear to have had influence only over part of Israel. We are given quite a bit of detail of some of them, while others are passed over in a verse or two and we are left puzzled as to what these actually did.

Through Judges 3-4 the periods of oppression get longer. First Othniel deals with the oppressor in battle. After that King Eglon of Moab oppresses Israel and is dispatched by Ehud during a private interview when Ehud made effective use of his two edged sword. These are not tales for the squeamish!

Then Israel is oppressed by Jabin, King of Hazor from the north. Yes, we thought we had seen the last of him in Joshua 11. It is entirely possible that in the considerable time interval since then Hazor could have been rebuilt. Also royal families do have a tendency to be lacking in originality in their use of names. Here a prophetess, Deborah takes the lead in inspiring Barak to fight Sisera, Jabin's commander. A great rain storm during the battle put Jabin's crack chariot force out of action.

Chariot wheels do not run very well over soggy ground! Remember that the Creator is in charge of His creation!

The method by which Sisera was despatched violated all norms of Ancient Near Eastern hospitality, but in the circumstances one can understand the Israelites' joy at being free from the oppressor and their lack of scruple as to how this had been achieved.

Israel's next lapse led to constant invasions by Midianite hordes who raided them, taking off livestock as well as ruining and pillaging crops. God called Gideon to deal with them, much to his surprise. He first had to clean up the worship in his own household. Gideon then got together a big army which God whittled down to three hundred men. Each was to be armed with a ram's horn trumpet, and a jar in which to conceal a lighted torch, the standard equipment of the leader of a band of men. They encircled the Midianite camp at night and, at a command from Gideon, blew their trumpets and yelled, "A sword for the Lord and for Gideon." (Judges 7:20 ESV) They smashed their jars, thus exposing the lighted torches.

Waking in the middle of the night, the Midianites thought that they were surrounded by large numbers of the enemy who had arrived from nowhere. Gideon's men held their position while the Midianites, still half asleep, either fled or fought each other and then Gideon pursued them.

Sadly at the end of his life, Gideon used the gold plundered from the Midianites to make some sort of image which led to the Israelites worshipping it instead of the Lord. After his death the Israelites continued their round of idolatry, leading to oppression etc. One of Gideon's sons, Abimelech, wiped out the rest of the family to remove potential rivals to his position and, after a colourful career, eventually perished when a woman dropped a well-aimed millstone on his head.

Later on, when Israel was oppressed by the Ammonites, Jephthah, a man from Gilead, east of the Jordan, became their leader and successfully fought off the oppressor. We see what a low state Israelite religion had come to in that Jephthah vowed to the Lord that, if he won the battle, then he would sacrifice whatever, (and he must have meant whoever,) first came out of his house to greet him. This ignores the fact that the Law had made it perfectly clear that God hated human sacrifice and this practice was one of the reasons that He had judged the Canaanites. The sad story continues with the fact that Jephthah's only daughter was the first to greet him and so paid the price of this foolish rash vow.

The last named judge in the book is Samson. He is a bit like a perpetual problem teenager. His birth had been announced to his mother by an angel. She had also been told that he was to be under the Nazirite vow right from his birth and throughout his life. (For the regulations for this see Numbers 6). But the important thing here is that the Nazirite would never cut his hair while he was under his vow and so this meant that Samson's hair should never be cut during his lifetime. This symbolised his adherence to this vow of dedication to God.

The oppressors of Israel at this time were the Philistines who had recently settled in force on the southern coast of Israel, and had set themselves up there and tended to expand throughout the rest of Israel's territory. On the whole they were not treating the Israelites as badly as some of their other neighbours had done. There was even some danger that the two peoples would live alongside and that the more powerful Philistines might gradually absorb Israel.

Samson's provocative attitude saw to it that this danger at least was averted. He waged a one-man campaign against the Philistines. He never had an army. He did not even have the backing of the men of the tribe of Judah, who felt that he was just making trouble for them and were quite willing to tie him up and hand him over to the Philistines.

In the end Samson's latest love, Delilah, under great pressure from the Philistine rulers, lured from him the secret of his strength. His hair had never been cut. Remember this was the sign of his Nazirite vow. So Delilah arranged for a man to cut off his hair while he slept. Thus his vow was repudiated and his phenomenal strength gone. He was captured by the Philistines, blinded and set to work in a mill.

One day they chose to celebrate the capture of Samson, a victory as they saw it for their god, Dagon. Samson was to entertain them! For a while he obligingly performed for them. Then he asked to lean on the pillars of the rather unstable makeshift temple, in which and on which people were crowded. Suddenly Samson leaned forward with all his might and pulled it down, causing death and destruction amongst the Philistines as well as his own death. The Philistines were still going to dominate Israel for a good many years, but there was no risk of Israel just being quietly absorbed by them now.

The last five chapters of Judges must be recording about the lowest point in the religion and morality of Israel. The tribe of Dan migrated to the north of Canaan. There was a civil war with most of the Israelite tribes ranged against the tribe of Benjamin. Clearly Israel needed stronger visible leadership than the ad hoc system she had experienced thus far.

# *Loyalty and Faith: Ruth*

THE LITTLE BOOK OF RUTH gives us the very different picture of this period in Israel's story, showing that there were still those in Israel who took their faith in God as a guide to life. Naomi along with her husband, Elimelech, and their two sons go as temporary residents to Moab because of a famine in Israel. The two sons marry Moabite women, but one by one the menfolk in Naomi's family all die. She is about to return to Israel when Ruth, one of her Moabite daughters-in-law, declares that she will go with her, adopting both her people and her God.

When Ruth goes gleaning the grainfields after harvest she happens to go into the fields of Boaz, an upright man of some wealth, who is a relative of Naomi. He gives his reapers instructions not to harm her in any way and to make her work fruitful by even pulling out handfuls of the cut corn and leaving them for her to pick up. She is also invited to eat with his reapers. Throughout the book, God's over-ruling providence and care for these two widows is very evident.

In Israel if a man died without children his nearest male relative would have the responsibility of marrying the widow. Their first child would count as the child of the dead man and would inherit his property. Naomi tells Ruth to claim that Boaz fulfil this role for her and thus to keep Elimelech's property in the family. Boaz is willing to accept this and the book ends happily with a delighted Naomi holding her grandson, the child of Boaz and Ruth. He is an ancestor of Israel's greatest king, David.

# Eli and then Samuel: 1 Samuel 1-8

THE BOOK OF SAMUEL OPENS with Eli being both priest and judge/ruler of Israel probably early in the eleventh century BC. A man named Elkanah and his two wives come annually to the sanctuary at Shiloh to offer sacrifices. One of his wives, Hannah, who till then was childless, prayed for a son, promising to give him back to the Lord. Her prayer was answered in the birth of Samuel and when he was weaned, at anything from three to five years old, she did bring him back to the sanctuary and gave him to Eli. She saw him each year when she and her husband came to Shiloh to make their sacrifice. God gave her five other children.

(Interestingly enough Elkanah is the last example we have in the Old Testament of a commoner who had more than one wife. True we do not know much about the matrimonial status of most of the Israelites we read about, so maybe not much can be built on this. Israelite kings appeared to be well supplied with wives long after this time!)

Samuel's good progress is reported sandwiched in between accounts of the undisciplined and scandalous behaviour of Eli's two sons, Hophni and Phinehas, who were also priests. Thus the contrast between them stands out sharply.

The well known story of the night when God spoke to Samuel is frequently ripped out of its context! (The still, small voice speaking to Elijah and the call of Isaiah are other passages regularly treated in the same way!)

Yes, God spoke to Samuel. But what did God say to Samuel once He had got his attention? Samuel was told of the judgement which God would carry out on the house of Eli because of Eli's total failure to restrain his sons from evil. It actually came about like this.

The Israelites lost a battle against the Philistines. They decided that if they took the Ark of the Covenant into battle that would no doubt twist God's arm and persuade Him to give them victory. They had yet to learn that God is God and that He cannot be manipulated. Not only did they lose the battle with both Hophni and Phinehas, Eli's two sons, being killed, but the Ark of God was captured by the Philistines. When news of this came to Eli, he fell off his chair and broke his neck Other references such as Jeremiah 7:12-14 make it clear that the sanctuary at Shiloh was destroyed by the Philistines at the same time.

The Philistines then placed their great trophy, the Ark, in the temple of Dagon their god and set it beside his image. Once before they had come to grief celebrating what they saw as Dagon's triumph, but apparently they had not learnt from that occasion. Next day Dagon was found flat on his face on the ground before the Ark. So the Philistines stood him up. Next day he had fallen over again: worse still his head and hands had been broken off.

Then a plague broke out amongst the people of Ashdod where the Ark was, so the Philistines sent it on to Gath where the people panicked when they knew it was coming. Eventually the Philistines decided the Ark was too hot to handle, and too dangerous for them to keep, so the only thing to do was to send it back to Israel with what they saw as a suitable offering.

The Israelites rejoiced to have the Ark back, but they too didn't know what to do with it. Some, who totally disregarded all the laws concerning the Ark, looked into it and were put to death. So the Israelites too were finding it a danger when it was misused. So they left it in one of their cities and on the whole forgot about it for maybe up to half a century or so.

❧

Samuel succeeded Eli and became the last judge of Israel. One of his first actions was to call the Israelites together and to lead them to repent and to rid themselves of foreign gods and to confess their sins of idolatry to the Lord. For this they assembled at Mizpah. When the Philistines heard about this Israelite assembly they prepared to attack them. Samuel's role was to intercede for Israel. The Lord produced a mighty thunderstorm, throwing the Philistines into a panic. So this was another battle won other than by hard fighting. During Samuel's time Israel regained quite a bit of the territory which the Philistines had taken from her, but the Philistine threat was not finally removed in his lifetime.

❧

Samuel does not seem to have been much more successful as a father than Eli was, in spite of his having observed the consequences of Eli's failure. His own two sons were not shaping up as suitable leaders of Israel as they were unjust, dishonest and open to bribery. The leaders of Israel complained to Samuel about this and asked that a king be appointed for them like the other nations had. In particular, as they were very much aware of the continuing pressure from the Philistines and others, they wanted a king to lead them out into battle. Samuel clearly felt rejected by this request, but God told him to comply with it.

Samuel told the Israelites of the oppression and taxation a king could bring. Even that did not put them off the idea.

# Saul, Israel's First King:
# 1 Samuel 9-31

In the tribe of Benjamin there was a man, Kish, who had considerable standing in the community. His son was an impressive young man named Saul. When Saul was out looking for his father's lost asses, he came to Samuel to ask where they could be found. God had already told Samuel that Saul was the one he was to anoint as Israel's king, who would deliver Israel from the Philistines. So Samuel anointed Saul privately and told him that he was to be Israel's king. In spite of that Saul clearly did not feel ready for the job, so he hid when he was publicly chosen for this position!

Samuel explained the duties and regulations concerning the kingship to the Israelites. Yes, the Israelites' king would lead them in battle. But there were basic differences between kingship in Israel and kingship elsewhere in the Ancient Near East. The other kings were law-makers. Instead the kings of Israel had the responsibility of upholding the covenant law which Israel had been given at Sinai. Most important of all, they were to maintain the exclusive worship of the Lord as only then would the Israelites observe the rest of the law with its emphasis on the care of the less fortunate members of their society.

Saul's first military exploit, when he rescued the people of the town of Jabesh Gilead from the Ammonites, certainly showed that he had what it would take to lead Israel. At this point Saul has Samuel's whole-hearted support. So far so good.

But Samuel knew that the whole kingship idea was fraught with dangers for Israel so, as he was now handing over much of the leadership of Israel to Saul, he gave the Israelites a final warning against idolatry. (You will find out about the connection between kingship and idolatry later on in Israel's story!) But Samuel assured them that if both king and people followed the Lord then all would be well.

Saul soon finds that he is under pressure from the Philistines. They had a monopoly in the use of iron in the area in order to prevent the Israelites from making swords and spears. As a result of this Saul and his son, Jonathan, were the only Israelites equipped with these weapons. Samuel had instructed Saul to wait for him to come and offer the sacrifice before the battle. At the time Samuel should have come, Saul found his situation becoming more and more difficult with soldiers deserting in the face of an increasing Philistine force. So he offered the sacrifice himself and, of course, just at that point, Samuel appeared. Saul makes excuses for the way he had usurped the priestly function. Samuel is not impressed and announces to Saul that as a result of this he would not now found a dynasty in Israel. Instead God would choose a man 'after His own heart' to lead Israel.

Next the initiative of Jonathan, Saul's eldest son, leads to a resounding victory over the Philistines. But Jonathan then comes within a whisker of losing his life at his father's command! For Saul had imposed a foolish vow on his troops, banning them from eating anything till evening and thus weakening them for the battle! Jonathan did not hear of this until after he had helped himself to some wild honeycomb. Later, when Saul found out that his oath had been broken, he was prepared to have the culprit killed, even when it turned out to be Jonathan. Saul's soldiers, however, prevented this. This does raise questions about Saul's leadership.

But Saul did have another chance. He was commanded by God to carry out the sacred ban on the Amalekites, who had been long term enemies of Israel. He partially carried out this command, sparing the king and the best of the livestock, whose bleating gave him away as Samuel approached. Again Saul began to make excuses saying that he was under pressure from his men. He had a truly modern reluctance to take any responsibility for his actions.

Samuel could not go on supporting a king who disobeyed God's commands. This confrontation was their final meeting. The Israelite kingdom would be given to a better man than Saul. But Samuel mourned for Saul, for what might have been, no doubt, and for what was lost in Saul's disobedience.

So this is where David first comes on the scene, when Samuel anoints him in secret in a private ceremony at his home in Bethlehem. God chose David. But remember God had also chosen Saul. Being chosen is only the first step; the chosen one must take full responsibility for what he does after that.

There is a warning for all in Saul's story. Continued disobedience to the Lord opens the door for enemy oppression. Instead of the Spirit of God being in charge of Saul now, an evil spirit came on him from time to time. Yes, the Old Testament says, 'from the Lord'. We read little about Satan and his activities in the Old Testament, though he was alive and active: what we really know about him comes from the New Testament. Instead, here in the Old Testament, everything is attributed to the Lord and certainly nothing could happen without His permission. So Saul had been making wrong choices and now there was an evil spirit backing up those wrong choices. This still does not make Saul the victim of his circumstances. In the Bible, so unlike our modern culture, people are held responsible for what they do. God still holds people responsible for their own actions and decisions whatever excuses they might try to make.

෴

David was sometimes employed as a musician to soothe Saul out of his dark moods. Somewhere along the line came his confrontation with Goliath the Philistine giant and his bold assertion that he came against him in the name of the Lord of Hosts who then gave him the victory. David's successes against the Philistines were celebrated in song by the Israelite women, who unwisely attributed ten times more success to David than to Saul. Saul then gave way to intense jealousy of David. This resulted in Saul having a series of attempts to assassinate David himself. Somehow the news of David's secret anointing may have reached Saul. In a fury he points out to Jonathan that if David lives, then it will be David and not Jonathan who would succeed him as king of Israel.

The relationship between David and Jonathan is not just a nice little friendship between two boys. It would appear that Jonathan was a good ten years senior to David. Further here in David was someone who excelled at those things Jonathan did best and who was going to be the next king instead of this rightful heir. So David's covenant with Jonathan had important provisions for the future in an age when it was not unusual for the new king to wipe out the previous king's whole family, thus removing the potential for rebellion and revolution.

The terms of this covenant, which can be found in 1 Samuel 20:14-15, were designed to protect the remaining family of either party in the event of the other reigning. So in his later attitude to Mephibosheth, Jonathan's son, David was carrying out the obligations he had agreed to in this covenant.

But there is no doubt that Jonathan's attitude to David was an extremely generous one and their friendship real. The last time they met we are told that Jonathan helped David to find strength in God. He also assured David that he would be the next king after Saul. That is quite something coming from the official heir to the throne!

For Saul now regarded David as his enemy and was using his army and country's resources to hunt David instead of dealing with the Philistines. Thus because of Saul's own wrong choice, the prophecy made just prior to his anointing, that he would deliver Israel from the Philistines, was not fulfilled. Saul even slaughtered the priests of the Lord at Nob because they had innocently given refuge to David. This was an appalling act of sacrilege by one who was himself some sort of believer in the Lord.

David lived as an outlaw with a band of rough men. Twice he had the opportunity to ssassinate Saul, but refused to touch one who was the Lord's anointed. More than once he took refuge amongst the Philistines as the only place of comparative safety from Saul and they assigned him the little town of Ziklag. He was with the Philistines when Saul prepared for his final battle with them and this put him in a difficult position. He would alienate the Israelites if he fought along with the Philistines, but to turn and fight with the Israelites would be an act of treachery to his host. The local Philistine king, Achish, was quite happy to have David go out with his commanders into the battle, but other Philistine leaders objected to this. So David was dismissed and this difficult choice was not left to him.

The Amalekites had raided Ziklag while David was away, and had taken the wives, children and property of David and his men. Whatever else was going on around him there was no time to lose, so David summoned his men to pursue the Amalekites. Thus while Saul fought his final battle against the Philistines, David was too busy retrieving all that the Amalekites had taken to have any part in it.

Around 1000 BC Saul faced the Philistine army on Mount Gilboa in central Israel. He had already been to the witch of Endor to consult the dead Samuel about this fateful battle and had been forewarned of disaster. Disaster came indeed as Jonathan and two of Saul's other sons were killed. Saul was so badly wounded that he killed himself to avoid falling helpless into Philistine hands. The Israelite army was heavily defeated. The Israelites fled from some of their towns in the vicinity of the battlefield and the Philistines occupied them. Israel was even more under the Philistine grip than when Saul took over some years earlier.

# David 2 Samuel

INITIALLY ISRAEL FELL APART AFTER this resounding defeat at the hands of the Philistines. David became king over the southern part of the country, that is, Judah. No doubt the Philistines didn't mind this too much. They had no reason to regard David as anything but a friend as they had given him refuge from Saul for some considerable time. Saul's army commander and relative, Abner, made Saul's remaining son, Ishbosheth, king over the north, Israel. It looks as though Ishbosheth was merely a puppet and Abner the real power in this area. For the country to be weak and divided suited the Philistines very well.

In your reading of what we are told in both books of Samuel about David, you might need to scrape off layers of church whitewash before you can find the real man, the one you will find in the actual Bible narrative. David is too often represented as a plaster saint, who yes, did have one lapse when he took Bathsheba, the wife of one of his outstanding soldiers, but he is frequently presented as something very far removed from the colourful character we actually have in the Bible.

There can probably be no doubt that David's mourning over Saul and Jonathan was sincere. For a while David only ruled over the south of the country from Hebron. But before long, Abner and Ishbosheth fell out and Abner decided that the time had come to throw his lot in with David and bring the rest of Israel with him. This left Ishbosheth in a hopeless situation. However, Joab, David's army commander had a feud to settle with Abner and soon assassinated him. Would Abner have been loyal to David or was he looking for power for himself? We shall never know.

David mourned Abner very publicly. Later two men came to David expecting a reward as they announced to him that they had murdered Ishbosheth. David expressed horror at this crime and had them put to death. David himself was almost certainly innocent in these cases, but these crimes were extraordinarily politically convenient and paved the way for him becoming king over all Israel within just over seven years after Saul's death.

A united Israel was exactly what the Philistines did not want. So there was an almost immediate confrontation with them and they were firmly put in their place by David and his men and had to settle back in their five cities with the surrounding countryside near the south west coast.

David's numerous other battles at last secured Israel's borders. In fact, in the absence of any great power dominating the Ancient Near East during that period, Israel was able to extend both her borders and her influence.

One masterstroke on David's part was to reconquer Jerusalem which had become a Jebusite stronghold again. Thus it became literally the city of David. It did not belong to any one of the twelve Israelite tribes so it did not arouse tribal jealousies. It made an excellent capital city especially as it was in an easily defensible position.

David brought the Ark of the Covenant to Jerusalem, thus making it also the religious centre for Israel. He wanted to build a temple for God there. Through the prophet Nathan, God told David that the temple would be built not by him, but by his son. However, David accumulated materials and drew up the plans for the temple in readiness for when his son would build it after his death. But God promised that He would build David a house, in the sense of an everlasting dynasty.

David's adultery with Bathsheba and the arranged death of her husband, Uriah, was an outrageous breach of covenant law, which was as binding on the king as on his subjects. It was not that David was short of wives at the time either. Quite early in his reign he already had at least half a dozen, which should have been quite enough to go on with! Once he was king over all Israel he had taken more wives and concubines.

But later when the prophet Nathan challenged David with his sin in this, he was ready to admit simply, 'I have sinned' and he made no excuses. This was the place Saul never really reached. By contrast Saul was always full of excuses for his failures: not his fault, someone pushed him. It is David's readiness to admit his sin when he saw it and to repent of it, that contributed to his being the man after God's own heart.

The area where David failed abysmally was in dealing with his sons. Don't think of an English nuclear family with mum, dad and a couple of kids as your model here! As you know David had plenty of wives before Bathsheba and also at least ten concubines. Actually bringing up the children would not be his responsibility along with running the country and fighting its wars. But he did need to deal with his sons' rivalries before they got too serious. Also he should have acted decisively when there was first the rape of his daughter, Tamar, by Amnon, her half brother, and then the murder of Amnon by Tamar's full brother, Absalom. Instead David just dithered. His own moral lapse had no doubt cost him his authority in these matters.

Absalom made the most of his opportunities of ingratiating himself with the common people. The day came when he proclaimed himself as king and so declared war on his father. David was totally unprepared for this in spite of the fact it had all been going on under his nose! He wisely decided to leave Jerusalem and so spare the city the horrors of a siege and also give himself time to muster some support in the country before a battle could take place.

As he fled the priests arrived, bringing with them the Ark of the Covenant. But David knew better than to treat this as a lucky charm. He was always ready to let God be God and told the priests to return the Ark to Jerusalem, pointing out that he was in God's hands. It was for God to decide whether or not he would return to Jerusalem as king.

Hushai, a friend of David's, pretended to desert to Absalom's camp in order to see if he could gain time for David. When Absalom's main adviser wisely counselled a swift attack on David before he had time to gather his forces, Hushai, using flowery language, countered this with advice to go far more cautiously. Hushai's advice prevailed and gave David much needed time.

When the armies were about to meet, David's men urged him not to go out with the troops as Absalom's men would be intent on killing him. So David's men went out under their commanders with the strictest instructions from David himself not to kill Absalom. Joab, David's long term commander, ignored this when he found Absalom hanging by his hair in a tree, after his mule had walked on. (Absalom had been inordinately vain about his exceptionally fine head of hair!) Joab was probably right in assuming that nothing would ever guarantee Absalom's loyalty to David after this whole episode.

David's excessive mourning over Absalom probably reflected the fact that he realised that this whole sorry episode in Israel's history was the result of his own failure to act. David got a sound ticking off from

Joab because he was mourning Absalom when he should have been congratulating his victorious troops. At least David did take notice of this and act on Joab's prompting.

Though David was restored as king over the whole of Israel, the fragility of the union of Israel and Judah had again been exposed. Then a Benjamite, that is a man from the same tribe as Saul, tried to foment another rebellion against David, but this was put down without shedding blood much beyond that of the rebel leader

Right at the end of David's life there was another crisis as he had failed to name his heir publicly and decisively. His eldest surviving son, Adonijah expected to succeed him and so did Bathsheba's son, Solomon. Adonijah, backed by Joab and the priest, Abiathar, got on with forwarding his claim and proclaiming himself king. Alarmed at this news Nathan, the prophet, prompted Bathsheba to tell the ailing David what had happened and to enquire whether he had not intended her son, Solomon, to reign. Bathsheba had acted in the nick of time and David made sure that Solomon was installed as his successor.

᪥

Why then did the Israelites look back to David as the ideal king? There was a great deal in his life which was flawed, far less than ideal. But David was loyal to God. No charge of idolatry was ever laid at his door. His bringing the Ark of the Covenant to Jerusalem and re-instating it would have been popular with the people. More importantly both that and his preparations for the building of the temple, showed the priority worship of the Lord had in his policy. Contrast this with Saul's neglect of the Ark and his slaughter of the priests at Nob.

Further David was always ready to acknowledge the sovereignty of God. Again when he had done wrong, he admitted this without excuse and repented whole-heartedly

Israel benefited enormously from the fact that under David she had secure borders for the first time in her history. After all, this was all happening in our world three thousand years ago and the Ancient Near East was usually in as much turmoil as it is now.

Finally we must not forget that God had promised that there would always be a descendant of David on the throne. If David had fallen short of being the ideal king in fact, then this descendant would not fail. He, God's Anointed One, the Messiah would establish God's reign of justice and righteousness for ever. But David himself had shown more interest in justice and righteousness than a good many of the kings who would come after him.

# Solomon: Wise Man or Fool?
## 1 Kings 1-11

SOLOMON BECAME KING AFTER DAVID around 960 BC. He began his reign with the problem of what to do with those who had supported Adonijah and whose loyalty was therefore suspect. Shimei, from the house of Saul, who had cursed David when he was retreating from Jerusalem was dealt with reasonably leniently at first, but severely when he transgressed the terms to which he had agreed. Even Adonijah's life was spared until he made it clear he had not given up ideas of gaining the throne!

Solomon began his reign asking God for the gift of wisdom and famously displaying this when he had to judge to which of two prostitutes a living child belonged and which one's child had died. However, he was not always wise in the way he ran the country and certainly not when it came to his matrimonial affairs.

His reputation for wisdom was partly based on his ability to produce songs and proverbs by the thousand! As these were largely about plant life, animals, birds, reptiles and fish, maybe natural history was his forte! Unfortunately wisdom did not always spill over into the practical affairs of his country as in the end, Israel, who really wanted another king like

David, decided categorically that she would not tolerate another one like Solomon!

He carried out the building of the temple delegated to him by his father. This was on roughly the same plan as the tabernacle before it, with the Holy of Holies, the Holy Place and then the outer courts. The whole scheme took seven years. But the construction of his own palace took thirteen years and that was not the only grandiose building for which he was responsible.

In fact Solomon's lavish building programme and luxurious court became a great drain on the nation's resources. Largely ignoring the old tribal boundaries, Solomon had the country divided into twelve districts for administrative purposes and each district had the onerous task of providing for his court for one month in rotation. The riches flowing into the kingdom were not sufficient to pay for everything. So Solomon ceded 20 towns in Galilee to Hiram of Tyre in payment for all the materials Hiram had sent him. (See 1 Kings 9:10-14) What would we think of a government which gave away the Isle of Wight to right its balance of payments deficit?

Native Canaanite peoples living in Israelite territory were pressed into slave labour on Solomon's various building projects. Solomon became middle man in a lucrative trade in chariots and horses.

Solomon inherited the Empire his father David had established. We have no record of him fighting any battles. But he did seek to cement relationships with Israel's neighbours by marriage alliances. This meant providing facilities for these foreign princesses to continue to worship their own gods. His biggest catch was Pharaoh's daughter for whom he built a special palace. He appears to have snapped up umpteen spare princesses, for he is credited with seven hundred wives and three hundred concubines. No wonder the upkeep of the court was a drain on the resources of the common people. Curiously enough, even with all that lot, we only ever read of one son for Solomon, Rehoboam by name. The dispute about the succession after his death was not a matter of sibling rivalry.

In lists later on we read of two people who each married a daughter of Solomon. And that is all we know about his children. Surely there were more than three!

So Solomon did make provision for his foreign wives to continue to worship their gods. This meant building shrines to other gods on Israelite territory and that surely infringed the Sinai Covenant. Joining in the worship of these gods, as Solomon did later on, certainly did. It was this activity that brought judgement on him: the loss of the whole northern territory to his descendants. Because of the promise God had made to David, He would not take the whole of Israel away from his descendants. But Solomon was told his son would only inherit one tribe, not the twelve.

Meanwhile Solomon had appointed an industrious young man, Jeroboam the son of Nebat, to be in charge of the forced labour of the tribe of Joseph. This meant that Jeroboam would be influential in a considerable section of the north of the country. One day, when he was out, he met the prophet Ahijah. Ahijah took off his own new cloak which he dramatically tore into twelve pieces, ten of which he gave to Jeroboam. The message was the same as the Lord's message had been to Solomon. Jeroboam would have ten tribes and one would be left to the house of David.

What about Ahijah's arithmetic? The tribe of Levi was probably not counted. They had been allotted forty eight cities with their pasture lands dispersed amongst the twelve tribes. But the division of Joseph into Ephraim and Manasseh meant that there were twelve tribes without Levi. However Simeon had settled in the middle of Judah and had scarcely been heard of since and had intermingled till it would have been hard to sort out! (Joshua 19:1) But the notion of twelve tribes lived on, even if it left Ahijah with one redundant piece of his cloak!

Solomon got wind of the meeting between Jerobaom and Ahijah and so Jeroboam fled to Egypt where he stayed until Solomon was dead. He then turned up where, from the point of view of Solomon's son, Rehoboam, he was least wanted. This was at the meeting of the Israelite elders which was called to confirm Solomon's son, Rehoboam as king.

For a around a hundred years, during the reigns of its first three kings, Saul, David and Solomon, Israel had been a united kingdom, more or less. Some of the cracks had been all too obvious at times in David's reign. Saul's court had been as modest as that of any of the judges, if not more so, while Solomon was heading for the style of an oriental despot. From being a people struggling for their national independence, Israel had become quite a power in the Ancient Near East. But now things were going to change. The days of the United Monarchy in Israel had come to an end in around one hundred years.

# The Division of the Kingdom: 1 Kings 12-16

ISRAEL HAD HAD ENOUGH OF Solomon and his extravagance. What she was not prepared to stomach was more of the same. When this was put to Rehoboam, Solomon's son, he totally misread the mood of the people and would make no concessions. This was Jeroboam's opportunity. He was already well known amongst the northern tribes and they opted to follow him and make him king, leaving Rehoboam with the tribe of Judah and part of Benjamin.

So the Israelite kingdom divided into two around 922 BC. The stronger kingdom economically was Israel in the north. But it was also more open to foreign influence and pressure than the south. It had no fixed capital at first, and its new king had little legitimate claim to the throne. However in that interview with Ahijah, Jeroboam had been promised that if he kept God's covenant, then God would give him a lasting dynasty. So it all depended on whether he was willing to take God's word seriously, where it always needs to be applied, that is in the practical issues of everyday life.

Judah in the south, tucked away in the mountains, was more isolated and poorer economically. But it had an excellent site for its capital city in Jerusalem. It also had the newly built temple and the advantage of the Davidic dynasty.

It is important to appreciate that from now on the two books of Kings alternate between what happened in Israel and what took place in Judah. The period of the Divided Monarchy is covered from 1 Kings 12 until 2 Kings 17. Of course in those days, nobody knew how far BC any of this was. So the only way of dating the king in one kingdom was by the reign of the king in the other. Kings weren't considerate enough to die conveniently at exactly the end of a year, so there are times when it is possible that the last half year or so of one king counts as the last year of his reign and the rest of that same year counts as the first year of his successor's reign. It's things like that which partly account for the fact that different calculations of dates around this period might vary a year of two, according to which book you are reading.

Most modern translations of the Bible do helpfully give a heading to each section of the text making it clear whether you are reading about Israel or Judah. After 2 Kings 17, when the Assyrians removed Israel from the map of the Ancient Near East, the story is inevitably going to be about Judah only.

Further there are the two books of Chronicles dealing with the whole period of the monarchy. That is relatively straightforward during the time when Israel was united. After that, the Chronicler is not interested in the north and only mentions it as it impinges on the story of Judah. His interest is God's king of the line of David, God's city, Jerusalem, God's temple, and God's law.

∽

The empire, built up by David and to some extent enduring under Solomon, began to fall away. United we stand, divided we fall. The two Israelite kingdoms spent too much of their time squabbling together and, if not doing that, Israel was often at war with Syria. Relations between these two were much as they are today, except that open hostilities were a great deal more frequent then.

Rehoboam's first reaction to the rebellion of the northern tribes was to muster an army to bring Israel to heel. Mercifully for once in his life he did take the right advice. Shemaiah, a prophet, warned him not to fight his brothers, the Israelites. To attempt to do so would have been suicidal. But shortly afterwards he was attacked by Shishak of Egypt who made off with much of the treasure from both temple and palace.

Remember that when God had first spoken to Jeroboam through Ahijah, He had promised that if he obeyed Him, then He would establish a lasting dynasty for him. Jeroboam was not the first or last man to fail because he did not trust what God had said to him. Suppose his people turned back to the house of David as a result of going up to Jerusalem to the temple? He worked out his own answer to that one. He set up golden bull images at shrines at Dan and Bethel, north and south of his country, and made these two places the main centres of worship. Maybe he had not intended outright idolatry, but the bull symbol was too intimately entwined with Baal worship ever to be safe in Israel, and outright idolatry was the result.

Jeroboam also built shrines for worship at the high places, that is, the hill tops where the Canaanites had worshipped Baal, and appointed priests who were not Levites and instituted a festival a month after the feast of Tabernacles. These religious innovations led to syncretism, that is, the mixing of religions, here that of the Canaanite gods with the worship of the Lord. All this was what the writer of the two Books of Kings calls the sin of Jeroboam with which he made Israel sin. Since all subsequent kings of Israel maintained this form of worship, all are dubbed guilty of the sins of Jeroboam

Why was idolatry regarded as such a serious offence by the writers of the OldTestament? There are several lines of approach here. In the worship of God the worshipper seeks to submit his will and his whole way of life to God. He exists to do God's will. But with idolatry, the aim is quite different. An idol must be manipulated, placated, persuaded to do the will of the worshipper. Worshippers here are interested only in what they will get out of it. It is their will which counts. (You will understand from this that there are subtle ways in which idolatry can creep into our churches and our own lives.) For that to which I look for the satisfaction of my needs is my idol, if it is anything but God Himself.

The worshippers of Baal and other Canaanite gods were intent on persuading Baal to give them good crops and enable their animals to breed well. Cult prostitutes, male and female, were readily available for the sexual rites accompanying this worship. those indulging in it were ignoring the fact that the Creator God was in charge of the whole agricultural cycle as well as everything else. Other gods were worshipped as well as Baal and child sacrifice was linked mainly with the worship of Moloch. So the problem was not simply that of a different form of service! Actually, apart from the gatherings for the annual festivals already mentioned, Israelite worship of the Lord took place in the family rather than in the community as a whole, at least until the introduction of synagogue worship during and after the exile.

There is another vital issue here. With this move away from covenant loyalty there was also inevitably a move away from covenant morality. Concern for justice and righteousness, care for the orphan, the fatherless, the widow and the foreigner would not survive the breakdown of covenant loyalty. When idolatry came in, morality went out of the door and usually quite fast. We see the same thing in our society today: the abandonment of the worship of God has led to the abandonment of moral standards.

⤸

An unknown prophet pronounced judgement on the altar at Bethel. Then Ahijah predicted judgement on Jeroboam. He would not now have any lasting dynasty. Indeed Jeroboam's son, who did succeed him as king, was assassinated in the second year of his reign and the assassin, Baasha, killed off the whole of Jeroboam's family, thus disposing of possible rivals. (You see the point of that earlier covenant between David and Jonathan!). The assassin's son succeeded him, but was likewise disposed of in the second year of his reign. This time the assassin, Zimri, reigned for a whole seven days, but that apparently gave him time to kill off Baasha's family!

Israel had descended into civil war from which the army commander, Omri, emerged as king. He greatest achievement was that he bought the hill of Samaria and built a city of the same name there, so at last the north had an easily defended capital. His reign is dismissed in a few verses, but later references to him in and out of the Bible showed that he made quite an impact on the whole area.

# Elijah and Israel's Crisis of Faith: 1 Kings 17-2 Kings 2

AHAB, OMRI'S SON, WHO REIGNED after him, married Jezebel of Tyre from Phoenicia. Jezebel came to Israel promoting her form of Baal worship with missionary zeal. Powerful, overbearing women are not an invention of the twenty first century. Here, three thousand years ago, Jezebel was the prototype and although queen consort and not herself the sovereign, she steered the rather weak Ahab as she would.

Israel's faith was now in severe crisis. She was being taught by Baal's prophets that she was to look to Baal for rain, crops, fertility. She was moving further and further away from her covenant with the Lord.

Then a prophet, one who delivers God's message, appeared on the scene. His name was  Elijah. He issued a stark warning to Ahab: that there would be neither dew nor rain in Israel until he said so! But rain, crops, fertility were Baal's special department. So all this was one in the eye for Baal. It would demonstrate Who really is in charge of creation. Even the prophet's name was a challenge to Baal. It meant the Lord is God so the implication was that Baal was not god. There is not room in the world for both!

After such a challenge to all that Jezebel held dear, Elijah had to make himself scarce. As commanded by God, he first of all lived near the Brook Cherith until it dried up. Then God told him to go to Zarephath in Phoenicia to live with a widow there. So while Jezebel scoured Israel searching for him, Elijah was living quietly near her own home patch outside Israel. Faith is like muscles in that it grows when you use it. These three years during the drought were the time when Elijah's faith grew as God provided for him, first through ravens bringing him daily food, and then as the widow's minute store of food was constantly renewed so that there was enough for her son and herself as well as Elijah. When the widow's son died, God used Elijah to restore him to life. So God gave Elijah three years' special training in trusting Him before the final showdown with the prophets of Baal.

After the three year drought and consequent crop failures, Israel was now in such straits that Elijah could tell Ahab what needed to be done. People from all over Israel were to be summoned to Mount Carmel, along with all the prophets of Baal and Asherah, whom Jezebel provided for at court. Elijah challenged the people to decide whether the Lord or Baal were God, but he received no answer. So it was agreed that both sides were to set up an altar with a sacrifice ready cut up on it. Whichever god answered by lighting the sacrifice was the real God.

Baal's prophets had first go, and though they appealed to Baal from morning till noon and then on till around three in the afternoon, they got no reply at all. Nothing happened as they got more and more frenzied.

Then Elijah had his turn. First of all he had his offering soaked in water. Then he appealed to the Lord, the God of Abraham, Isaac and Jacob to answer him so the onlookers would know He is God. Fire from the Lord fell and consumed the sacrifice completely. The Israelites immediately responded by acknowledging that the Lord, not Baal, is

God. But sadly this did not lead to any fundamental long term change in their loyalties or their lives.

At Elijah's command the prophets of Baal, who had been misleading the people, were rounded up and executed. All the obstacles to the ending of the drought had now been removed. So Elijah prayed to God to send the much needed rain. When a little cloud was seen in the distance, he ran ahead of Ahab's chariot all the way to Jezreel and a heavy rainstorm broke the drought.

Elijah was utterly exhausted. We have seen before that the moment of victory is often a very dangerous time spiritually. Jezebel heard of all that had happened and of the slaughter of her prophets and she vowed to deal in the same way with Elijah within the next twenty four hours.

Elijah fled south out of Israel and down through Judah to its southernmost point, where he sat down and wished himself dead. After all he had been no more successful in turning Israel back the Lord than had his predecessors before him. He slept and when he awoke an angel came to him and provided food and water for him. He slept again and again the angel provided food and water. Then he went on to Horeb, the mountain of God where God had given the Sinai Covenant to Moses. (There is some discussion as to whether the terms Horeb and Sinai are interchangeable or whether Horeb was a particular peak in the Sinai range.)

The Lord asked Elijah what he was doing there. His reply accused the Israelites of breaking God's covenant, destroying His altars, killing His prophets. Elijah felt he was the only loyal prophet left and he knew that his own life was in danger. Then there is the famous passage about God not being in the wind, earthquake or fire, but in the gentle whisper which came to Elijah. Unfortunately all the sermons I have ever heard on it stop there and ignore what that gentle voice said. It was also a very firm voice!

After asking Elijah the same question again and eliciting the same reply, God then told him to return the way he came! He was given three tasks. One was to anoint Hazael as King of Syria, another to anoint Jehu as King of Israel and the third was to anoint Elisha as his own replacement. In the event the first two of these tasks were carried out by Elisha.

❧

King Ahab fancied growing his own vegetables! (And that even without Jamie Oliver and all the publicity about healthy eating!) The ideal plot for this, close to his palace, was the vineyard belonging to a man called Naboth. Ahab should have known very well that covenant law forbad a person to part with his family inheritance of land. But, in spite of this, he offered Naboth either an exchange of a better vineyard or the value of his current vineyard. Naboth quite rightly refused and there the matter ought to have stopped. But for Jezebel's intervention it would have stopped there.

Not for the first time, Ahab responded with a fit of the sulks hardly suitable for his royal position! So Jezebel sorted out the situation her way. Covenant law and the protection of the ordinary people meant nothing to her. You get what you want however you can. So she arranged a mock trial at which Naboth was falsely accused of cursing God and the king and was taken out of the city and stoned. Triumphantly she announced to Ahab that he could now take the vineyard as Naboth was dead.

Ahab went down to view his new acquisition and there was the last person he wanted to meet - Elijah. God had told him to go down to the vineyard to meet Ahab and to pronounce judgement on him and his house. He did just this. Where the dogs had licked Naboth's blood they would also lick Ahab's and they would, in fact, devour Jezebel.

❧

After an apparently unusual situation of three years with no war between Israel and Syria, Ahab of Israel and Jehoshaphat of Judah decided to join forces to recover the city of Ramoth Gilead from Syria for Israel. But first they wanted prophetic confirmation that this would be successful. Jehoshaphat was remarkably sceptical about the glib optimism of the four hundred prophets whom Ahab had consulted. He insisted that another prophet, named Micaiah, also be asked for the word he was getting. Ahab complained vehemently that Micaiah always prophesied something bad for him. Anyway Micaiah was consulted and, in spite of efforts to intimidate him, he made it clear that Ahab would fall in battle. So in order to nullify the prophecy, Ahab went into battle in disguise. However, a chance arrow found him and he died of his wound that day and his son, Ahaziah became king.

Somehow Ahaziah was then careless enough to fall through the latticed window of his upper room in Samaria and he was injured to a point where it was clear that his life was in danger. So he sent a messenger to enquire of Baal-zebub, the god of Ekron, as to whether he would recover or not. This was an affront to the Lord. Ahaziah was behaving as if there were no God in Israel.

❧

So God sent Elijah to intercept the messenger and tell him that the king would not recover. If you don't like the message, then go for the messenger! That seems to be the policy here, as Ahaziah sent three squads of men to arrest Elijah. The first two met a quick end and the third approached humbly and implored Elijah to accompany him back to Ahaziah, which he did and there repeated his message to the king.

# Elisha and the
# Prophetic Revolution 2 Kings 2-13

AFTER THIS, WHILE ELIJAH AND Elisha were together, a chariot and horsemen of fire separated them one from the other and Elijah was taken up in a whirlwind into heaven. Just before this, when offered one request from Elijah, Elisha had asked for a double portion of his spirit. He is not saying, "I want to be twice as good as you were!" What he is saying is, "Let me be your true son and heir". So the task of challenging Baal worship and all its effects now fell on Elisha.

Elisha had quite a varied ministry. He certainly had compassion and concern for individuals in need. One example of this is the widow for whom God gave a miraculous provision of olive oil for her to sell in payment of her debts and so saved her two sons from slavery

Elisha often stopped to have a meal with a wealthy Shunammite woman and her husband. The woman suggested that they make him a little furnished bed-sit on the roof. So they built a roof room  and equipped it  with a lamp, bed, table and chair. Elijah told them that they would have a son. Some while later on a very hot day this cherished son died, maybe from sunstroke. The distressed mother sought out Elisha who came and raised the child back to life.

When the Syrian commander, Naaman who suffered from some form of leprosy, came to the king of Israel, mistakenly thinking that he had miraculous healing powers, Elisha heard of it and asked that Naaman be sent to him. Naaman was told to wash himself seven times in the River Jordan and he would be healed as indeed he was. His response was to proclaim that he now knew there was no God in all the earth but in Israel. But what was he to do back in Syria? This was his first moment of faith, before he had time to think it all through. So he asked for two mules' loads of Israelite soil to take back with him, so that he could henceforth worship Israel's God on Israelite soil even though he was in Syria!

Elisha had refused the lavish gifts offered him by Naaman: God's gifts cannot be purchased or paid for. But the temptation was too much for Elisha's servant, Gehazi. The judgement on him was that he could have Naaman's leprosy as well as Naaman's goods.

On more than one occasion Elisha proved to be a useful person to have with the army camp! When the armies of Israel, Judah and Edom were fighting against Moab, they faced disaster because they had run out of water. Through the word of God given to him, Elisha told them to dig ditches in the valley where they were camped and that in the morning these would be full of water, which flowed into them from the hills of Edom where there was heavy overnight rain.

Later when Israel and Syria were in their usual state of hostilities, the king of Syria was sure there was a traitor in his camp because his plans were constantly being revealed to the other side! But what was happening was that God told Elisha what the Syrians were about to do and Elisha told the king of Israel. Once informed that this was what was happening, the King of Syria sent a force to capture Elisha. Seeing this army surrounding them, Elisha's servant panicked. Elisha's calm answer was that those on his side were the more numerous and he prayed to God to help the servant see the real situation: that they were protected by chariots and horses of fire. Elisha was able to ward off this Syrian attack as the Lord struck the Syrian soldiers with blindness and Elisha then led them right into Samaria where he prayed that the Lord would open their eyes. He prevented the King of Israel from killing them, persuaded him to give them food and drink and send them home. That bought a temporary peace.

It was only temporary. The Syrians raided Israel and laid siege to Samaria where people began to starve. The King reasoned that if Elisha had not previously insisted on releasing the Syrian army, then this could not have happened and so he swore that he would remove Elisha's head from off his shoulders that day, though it is difficult to see how this would have helped the situation for anyone. At the same time God revealed to Elisha that within twenty four hours food would be readily and cheaply available in Samaria.

At dusk four men with leprosy, who therefore were not allowed in the city but camped at its gates, decided to go and surrender to the Syrians in the hope that this way they would get fed. But when they got to the Syrian camp they found it deserted. God had caused the Syrians to hear a noise like that of horses and chariots and so they had assumed a great force was coming against them and had fled in panic. All their stuff was left behind. The four men ate and drank their fill and then carried off silver and gold and clothing to hide.

Then they paused and decided the good news must be made known to the King of Israel. At first he was reluctant to believe them, but the Syrian camp was found just as the four men had described it. So the starving people in Samaria had food and plenty of it and Elisha's head remained where it always had been!

❦

Elisha told one of the prophets who were around him to go to the Israelite army at Ramoth Gilead and to get the commander, Jehu, on his own. The prophet was then to anoint him as king of Israel and immediately afterwards to run for it! This done, Jehu's men readily proclaimed him king.

The first thing Jehu did was to confront the rightful king of Israel, King, Joram. King Ahaziah of Judah was visiting Joram who was recovering from a battle wound. So Jehu killed both monarchs! (You did notice, didn't you, that this is Ahaziah of Judah. The Ahaziah of Israel of whom you read a few pages back had died as Elijah said he would. You might be feeling that it is a pity there was this apparent shortage of names in royal circles in both Israel and Judah.)

Jehu then went on to Jezreel to deal with the Queen Mother, Jezebel. She did herself up like the dogs' dinner and, after Jehu had ordered her to be thrown down out of the window, that is in fact just what she became, exactly as Elijah had prophesied!

As a usurper on the throne, Jehu now had one interest and that was how to keep Jehu in power. So all the house of Ahab and the supporters of the Tyrian Baal, all those who had been connected with the previous regime and therefore might plot against Jehu, were slaughtered one way or the other. This did get rid of the Tyrian Baal and of any potential opposition to Jehu. But he was not interested in cleaning up Israel's worship and sorting it out from that of the Canaanite Baal. Like all the kings of Israel he followed the religious pattern set by Jeroboam I.

With the murder of her king, the crisis affected Judah as well. There the Queen Mother was Athaliah, a daughter of Jezebel and very much a chip off the old block. When she heard that her son had been murdered she attempted to wipe out the whole Davidic line and take over Judah for herself. But a sister of the dead king managed to smuggle away one young prince and bring him up secretly over the next six years, while Judah endured Athaliah's reign. Then Jehoiada the priest staged a well planned coup which placed the young prince, Joash, on the throne of Judah and Athaliah was put to death. In the end Joash too was assassinated, but not till he had reigned for forty years.

Intermittent war with Syria continued to weaken both of the Israelite kingdoms. Joash's son, Amaziah, reigned for twenty-five years before he too was assassinated. He had foolishly begun a war against Israel which would further weaken both kingdoms, especially his own.

# The Eighth Century Prophets: Amos, Hosea in Israel

### and the end of the Northern Kingdom
### (see also 2 Kings 14-17 for the end of Israel)

EARLY ON IN THE EIGHTH century BC both Israel and Judah entered in to a period of greater stability. King Azariah, otherwise known as Uzziah, reigned in Judah and Jeroboam II was king in Israel. Both had unusually long reigns. There was a bit of a power vacuum in the Ancient Near East at the time and so neither kingdom was experiencing much external threat. Both kingdoms became more prosperous, or at least, some people within them did, and that often at the expense of the poor. This again was a fundamental breach of covenant law.

Four great prophets stand out in the eighth century BC They are Amos, Hosea, Isaiah and Micah. The first two directed their message to Israel and the other two mainly to Judah. So Amos is the first of the so-called 'Writing Prophets' which does not mean that previous prophets could not write. It means that Amos was the first prophet where we have a book of his prophetic oracles.

Elijah and Elisha, in the previous century, that, of course, was the ninth century BC, did not have their sayings collected in a book, but we

99

read about what they did in the books of Kings. Consequently we know more of their works than their words. It is the other way round with the eighth century prophets: we know their words, but not a great deal about anything else that they did.

The prophets were God's spokesmen. They spoke God's word into the situation in which they found themselves. Sometimes that word related to the more distant future, but almost always it had a direct relevance to the situation in which the prophet lived. Thus the prophet's message holds up God's mirror on society. Too often Christians have regarded the prophets' message simply as a quarry from which to cut out the gems of Messianic prophecy and then they choose to ignore the rest. That rest is of critical imprtance and can tell us what God thinks of our society and culture today. The principles informing the prophetic message have permanent relevance. Read the book and Amos and you could be reading about modern Britain!

Amos actually lived just over the border in Judah, but he went to Bethel in Israel to deliver his prophetic message. It was largely a message of judgement on a complacent, unjust, corrupt and idolatrous society. That sounds modern enough, too modern for comfort! Since he had a clear grasp that the Lord is God of the nations, he first of all pronounced judgement on Israel's neighbours for their inhumanity to each other, especially in warfare. As the Lord is God of the nations, so He is also Judge of the nations. They were to be judged according to the light they had. Only Judah was charged with breaking God's law because only Judah amongst Israel's neighbours had that law.

Amos charged the Israelites with numerous breaches of covenant law, especially taking advantage of the poor and selling them into slavery for small debts. They were keeping overnight garments given as a pledge for debt, that is the outer cloaks which doubled up as blankets. But, in order to avoid hardship to the poor, the law stated these garments must be returned to their owners at sunset. The better-off Israelites were warping the whole judicial process with bribery and corruption .

Yes, God had brought Israel out of Egypt, but privilege carried responsibility. The luxurious way of life of Israel's upper class would come to an end at the hands of Assyria. God wanted, not Israel's constant presence at the various shrines where worship was mixed up with Canaanite rites, but practical justice and righteousness in daily relationships. That, and that alone, would satisfy God, then and now.

With that justice and righteousness not forthcoming, the only remaining prospect for Israel would be God's judgement. Those who refused to hear God's word would suffer a famine of God's word. Just at the end of the book there is the promise of brighter days ahead, but that would be after the Assyrian attack, not before.

If Hosea's ministry overlapped at all with that of Amos, it certainly went on beyond it into the unstable period in Israel after the death of Jeroboam II. Israel had her last six kings in around thirty years. For some of these their main claim to the throne was responsibility for the assassination of their predecessor.

Unlike Amos, Hosea was a northerner, so he was preaching to his own people. His own personal experience coloured his message, perhaps that was one reason God chose him. For Hosea had an unfaithful wife, who ended up in the slave market, from which he bought her back. God showed Hosea how his own experience illustrated that of God with Israel, who was bound to Him by the covenant which she continually broke. As a marriage relationship is exclusive, so the relationship between God and Israel should have excluded all other gods. But you know the story so far and yet God had not given up on Israel as He had had every right to do on so many occasions.

So one of the important threads in Hosea is the emphasis on covenant loyalty, steadfast love, the attitude of constant love, loyalty and affection which one partner in a covenant should show towards the other. This quality of constancy and practical love is captured in the Hebrew word 'hesed'. God was showing that attitude even though Israel was not.

Hosea is clear enough that, with no repentance forthcoming, God would judge Israel. But he could not see the whole matter ending there. Beyond that judgement there would be room for a new beginning. Israel who had chased after the Baals, thinking that they supplied her needs, would at last be betrothed to her God in righteousness and justice, love and compassion, faithfulness and she would have a real relationship with her God.

As Israel got weaker, Assyria got stronger and the power vacuum of the first part of the eighth century was rapidly filled by its growing empire and ambition. Seeing the threat, Israel tried playing Egypt and Assyria off against each other, a policy which could only lead to disaster. The Assyrians came against Israel and besieged Samaria, which capitulated around 721B.C. That was the end of the Old Testament Northern Kingdom of Israel.

Many Israelites were taken by the Assyrians and forcibly settled in various parts of their empire. Peoples from different parts of the Assyrian Empire were brought to live in Israel. No doubt these were very unwelcome at first, but later on the Israelites inter-married with them. The resulting mixed population are the Samaritans we meet in the New Testament, those half-breeds despised by pure bred Jews! There was no widespread return of exiles from the Assyrian Empire to the area which had been the Northern Kingdom of Israel.

So for the rest of the Old Testament story, from 721 BC onwards, you will be reading about Judah, the Southern Kingdom only. It was all that was left. The northern kingdom, Israel, was no more.

# The Eighth Century Prophets: Isaiah and Micah in Judah

THE TWO ISRAELITES KINGDOMS TOGETHER had been an area around the size of Wales. Now that Israel, by far the larger of the two, had fallen to the Assyrians, the area left was small indeed and appeared to be at the mercy of the Assyrians.

As for observance of covenant law, Judah had not been doing quite as badly as Israel since the division of the kingdom. After all, she had some things which made for greater stability. She had the Davidic monarchy, all except for that brief period when Athaliah had usurped the throne. She had Jerusalem as her capital and the Temple as her centre or worship. Yes, her worship did get contaminated by rites of Canaanite Baal and this always led to loosening of moral standards. But unlike Israel, in between times, Judah did have a number of reforming kings, who sought to recall her to the ways of God, although usually they did not go so far as to wipe out the shrines on the high places where Baal was worshipped.

Politics and religion got mixed in the wrong way. If Judah made an alliance with an outside power, that involved some acknowledgement of the gods of that power. If another power held her as a tribute paying vassal, then she was expected to acknowledge the gods of that power.

Either way, her religious and moral life was compromised (There is a right way for politics and religion to mix. If political life were informed by God's word, then there would be some hope that the problems facing humanity could be usefully addressed. While God is excluded from such counsels, the political sphere is doomed to futility.)

❧

So Judah was very much under Assyria's thumb at the time when Hezekiah became king towards the last quarter of the eighth century BC. He was for shaking off the Assyrian yoke and reforming Judah's religious life. He did away with the high places. Some way through his reign the Assyrians marched out to attack Jerusalem. Judah's fortified cities fell to Assyria. Sennacherib of Assyria boasted that he had shut Hezekiah up in Jerusalem like a bird in a cage. Jerusalem was facing the prospect of a siege and worse, as the Assyrians made their triumphant way through Judah.

The Assyrian field commander approached Jerusalem with a message from their king, self styled the Great King. He questioned the value of Judah's alliance with Egypt, who was notoriously unreliable. He boasted of the way in which he had captured other countries and their gods. So, he claimed, he would go on to capture Jerusalem as the Lord would be no more able to deliver her than the gods of the other nations had been. In this boast he made a fundamental mistake.

Hezekiah sent for Isaiah the prophet, who announced that there was no need to fear the Assyrian, whose servants had blasphemed God by putting Him on a level with the gods of the nations. A little later on the Assyrian sent Hezekiah a letter boasting of their successes and again claiming that God, like the gods of the nations he had already conquered, could do nothing against the might of Assyria. Hezekiah spread the letter out before the Lord and prayed to Him for deliverance in order that the nations might recognise Him as God. (That's a splendid example of what to do with an unpleasant letter.)

Isaiah then sent a message to Hezekiah to the effect that Jerusalem could afford to despise and mock the Assyrian who had dared to insult the Holy One of Israel. Assyria's boasted conquests had been planned and permitted by God, otherwise they would not have happened. Assyria would be taken back to its own land with a hook in its nose, that is, like a prisoner of war! The Assyrians would not enter Jerusalem or even shoot an arrow against it.

That night an enormous number of men in the Assyrian camp died. An attack was no longer possible, and the rest of the army returned home. Sennacherib was later assassinated by his sons. Boastful, bully world powers, please note!

So, as Isaiah had said, God had delivered Jerusalem on this one occasion. Unfortunately many in Judah took this to mean that come what may, God would always deliver Jerusalem. After all, He needed the temple didn't He? Well they would find out the answer to that one later on!

Isaiah's message is mainly to Judah, though he began preaching before the fall of Samaria. Only a few messages are addressed particularly to the north. Isaiah's call in the year that King Uzziah died impressed upon him the holiness of God, who was the real King of the whole earth. Isaiah was to call on Judah to repent, but as they refused to do so, they would become deaf to prophet's message.

Isaiah challenged Judah to choose whether to trust in God or in Assyria for their security. Just after the call narrative in Isaiah 6 there is the example of Ahaz, a king who turned to Assyria for help and by contrast, at the end of this whole section, the story of Hezekiah, the king who did trust God for aid against Sennacherib of Assyria, is retold in Isaiah 36-37.

In fact the nations to whom Judah might turn for help are all under the judgement of Judah's God. They had nothing of worth to give Judah while she had the One they all needed most! Yet Isaiah knows that the real danger for Judah is not Assyria, but Babylon. Assyria would not conquer Judah, but Babylon would. Isaiah looks forward to a time when the exiles of Judah would be freed from Babylon.

He dares to state that the God of a tiny nation, whose defeat he could foresee, is in fact, the Lord of all nations and the Creator of the ends of the earth. He will restore His people from exile in Babylon back to their own land. Yes, God does things like that in human history.

❦

So many modern Christians have a pint sized god who has lost his grip on this world if he ever had much grip. Here is the prescription to cure that sub-Christian mentality. Read Isaiah 40 slowly twice a day for a fortnight. Don't dilute its message. Follow that up by reading all the rest of Isaiah. Let your concept of God expand to true biblical proportions.

❦

Like Amos, Isaiah is clear that God wants practical justice and righteousness in everyday life from His people. Religious performances were totally unacceptable if these moral qualities were lacking. Judah's religion was diluted by a mixture of Canaanite practices. If you ever want to know what God thinks about inter-faith worship, consider carefully what the prophets had to say about it. Remember that inevitably it involves demoting God down to the level of other so-called gods.

Unlike Amos and Hosea his near contemporaries, Isaiah speaks of a king from the line of David whose rule will exemplify all that justice and righteousness which God requires. Later he speaks of the Servant of the Lord, who though innocent, will die as a criminal and bear the sin of many. He does not appear to equate these two figures, but in the

New Testament, Jesus does so, as He is the fulfilment of both these lines of prophecy.

✍

The fourth of the eighth century prophets whose oracles are found in an Old Testament book is Micah. His message is delivered to both Judah and Israel, often concentrating on the two capitals, Jerusalem and Samaria. His prophecy is an indictment of the syncretistic worship, which mixed rites of the Lord and the Baals and the resulting laxity regarding covenant law. He condemns the greed and covetousness of those with the power to make themselves rich at the expense of the poor. He is prepared to take on any class of people, from the leaders of Israel to the false prophets.

Micah included a judgement oracle which many in his day would find unthinkable. Jerusalem would become a ploughed field, a heap of rubble. Later in Jeremiah 26:17-19 we read that this prophecy had motivated Hezekiah's reforms. So Micah's word did lead to the repentance of at least one king and gave Jerusalem a longer breathing space in which she could have put her house in order had she chosen to do so.

# *Judah in Crisis: Jeremiah.*

AFTER HEZEKIAH'S DEATH, JUDAH WAS ruled for over half a century by his son, Manasseh. This, the first half of the seventh century, was a time of Assyrian ascendancy and Manasseh was very much under the Assyrian's thumb. But he took idolatry in Judah to new levels and once ingrained in the people, it took the exile to erase it.

Manasseh restored the high places which Hezekiah had destroyed and re-introduced the worship of Baal and Asherah and built altars to the sun, moon and stars in the temple courts. He indulged in all kinds of occult practices, sorcery, divination, consulting mediums and spiritists. He also sacrificed his own son. Injustice was the inevitable fruit of this performance and many innocent people suffered at his hands. His son followed in his footsteps and was murdered after a couple of years' reign and he was succeeded in 640 BC by the eight year old Josiah.

Josiah sought to reverse the policy of his father and grandfather. When the temple was being sorted out, the high priest, Hilkiah, told Shaphan, the secretary that he had found the Book of the Law in the temple. Shaphan reported the find to the king, and read from it in his presence. Josiah was distressed and appalled to realise how far Judah had gone against the Law of God and so he sent a group of men, including Shaphan's son, Ahikam, to enquire from God concerning this.

It would appear that they could choose to whom they would go and they consulted a prophetess named Huldah. Her message was that the Lord would bring disaster on Jerusalem because of her idolatry just as the Book of the Law indicated. However, because of Josiah's repentant attitude and desire to obey God, this would not happen in his lifetime.

Josiah was anything but complacent about the message he received. He did all in his power to turn Judah back to God. He called the leaders of Judah and her priests and prophets together and read the book to them and then renewed the covenant to follow the Lord. He began a thorough-going purge of the idolatry in Jerusalem and Judah, beginning with the removal from the temple of those idolatrous objects introduced by Manasseh. Places of idolatrous worship were then desecrated.

As Assyria was now loosing its grip on the outlying parts of its empire, Josiah went beyond the borders of Judah into what had been Israel and continued his campaign there. He also got rid of occult practitioners. He ordered a great Passover celebration throughout his territory. There was little more he could have done. But the reforms did not change the hearts and lives of the people of Judah. After Josiah was tragically killed in the battle of Megiddo by the Egyptians in 609 BC, many in Judah returned to the idolatry with which they were all too familiar.

The prophet Jeremiah had been called to his daunting task about eighteen years before Josiah's death. Quite how he related to Josiah's reformation is an open question as he does not directly mention it. But he clearly states his respect and appreciation of Josiah as one who did what was just and right and defended the cause of the poor and needy:

conduct which was evidence of a relationship with the Lord. (Jeremiah 22:15-16)

Jeremiah was given a hard task. In his day the inhabitants of Jerusalem believed that as God had protected them from Sennacherib a century or so earlier, so He would ever protect them. After all, His temple was in Jerusalem and He couldn't do without that, could He? They also had the Davidic monarchy, along with the promise that there would always be a descendant of David on the throne of Jerusalem. So one way and another, whatever they did, they felt pretty secure. Jeremiah had to preach against that false security. God needed the temple in Jerusalem no more than he had needed the shrine at Shiloh which had been destroyed when Eli's sons were killed in battle around five hundred years earlier. The problem was Jeremiah saw this and the inhabitants of Judah and Jerusalem did not and would not. They felt as safe as the passengers on the ill-fated Titanic.

Like Hosea before him, Jeremiah often spoke of Judah's unfaithfulness to her covenant with the Lord as if she were an unfaithful wife. He repeatedly warned that such conduct would lead to the invasion of Judah by the Babylonians and to exile for many of the Jews.

Great empires came and went like mushrooms in the Ancient Near East, (those gorgeous big field mushrooms which can reach the size of a tea plate in a matter of days.) Perhaps great powers in our day would learn a little humility if they knew the Old Testament story, as God is no more likely to tolerate their pride than that of these ancient empires. Nineveh, the capital of Assyria, had been sacked in 612B.C. and the new super-power on the scene was Babylon. For a while Egypt was disputing who had influence at the eastern end of the Mediterranean, but she was not going to challenge Babylon seriously for long.

In fact Jeremiah saw Nebuchadnezzar of Babylon as God's servant carrying out His judgement on His people. Since they would not repent, their best policy would be to submit to the Babylonians when they came. That at least would have lessened the destruction the enemy would carry out.

But however often he repeated this, judgement at the hand of Babylon was not the whole of Jeremiah's message. Beyond the judgement and exile the Jews could hope to return to their own land after around seventy years. Then, purified by what they had been through, the Jews could seek God with all their hearts and find Him. Their city would be rebuilt on its ruins. They could start again. God had not given up on them. He never did. He would even make a new and better covenant with His people.

Jeremiah also includes oracles of judgement on the nations. They too were answerable to God for what they did. Babylon comes in for a specially lengthy oracle of judgement and the fulfilment of this would be the opportunity for the exiles to flee from her.

If you read the book of Jeremiah..... No, I mean when you read the book of Jeremiah, (and of course, there is no other way of either knowing or forming any opinion about its content!) you will find that this prophet is anything but the old misery so many people make him out to be. He was a man who loved his own people passionately, who was torn apart by the judgement that he knew would come on them for their disloyalty to God. For forty years he persevered in delivering this unpopular message. How did he keep going?

When it all got too much for him, he then told God exactly how he felt about it with an openness and honesty from which we can learn much. He had a strong relationship with God which meant he did not have to pussyfoot around, but he could say it just how he felt it. This freedom in his relationship with God would have done much to enable him to go on, when so many were against him, plotting his death, putting him in the stocks and then in prison.

❧

So after the battle of Carchemish in 605 BC (Jeremiah 46:1-2), it was Babylon rather than Egypt who had influence over Judah. In the aftermath of that battle some of the princes of Judah and young men of good family were taken to the Babylonian court and were to be trained for service there. Amongst these was a young man named Daniel and his three friends. The book of Daniel tells of their resolute faith in an alien culture and environment, even if this loyalty was going to mean death.

But the book of Daniel also shows the frailty of the great men of this world. We see the lack of trust between Nebuchadnezzar and his closest advisers when he orders them to interpret his dream and the way in which he is almost beside himself with anger as they are unable to do this. Later Belshazzar is wining and dining in careless ease while the enemy is nearing the city gates. On seeing a hand write on the wall, he becomes pale, his knees knock and his legs give way. Even Darius, who appears to be a more sympathetic character, is trapped in his own legislation.

This book of Daniel has suffered multitudes of strained and strange interpretations over the years, but a few things are certain. It tells of God as supreme over the kingdoms of the world. He, who is the Most High, rules and gives these kingdoms to whom He will. He is working out His purpose and the oppressor and persecutor will find, in the end, that their day was short.

❧

The Babylonians did invade Judah. In 598/7 BC. Jehoiakim, the king died and Jehoiachin was made king. He had no opportunity to deal with the crisis facing his country. Within three months he was captured and taken as an exile to Babylon along with some others of the royal family, the leaders of the people, the craftsmen and the soldiers. Many of the temple utensils also were taken to Babylon. Having removed those in leadership or with outstanding ability, the Babylonians hoped they had removed those capable of rebellion.

# *Among the Exiles: Ezekiel*

AMONGST THIS BATCH OF EXILES was a man from a priestly family named Ezekiel. Far from the Jerusalem temple, his prospects of entering the hereditary priesthood at thirty years old, as would have been normal back in Jerusalem, had been dashed. But at about the time when this should have happened in ordinary circumstances, God called him to be his prophet.

So Ezekiel was living in Babylon at the time when, though the king of Judah had been taken captive, the Babylonians had left Jerusalem more or less intact. The city with its temple was still standing. A new king of the Davidic line, Zedekiah was over what was left of Judah. So this was fertile ground for false prophets to regard what had happened as a kind of blip. In a couple of years all this would be over. The exiles would return to Jerusalem and life would go on again much as it had done. So much for Jeremiah's prophecies!

Nebuchadnezzar did catch a couple of these prophets who were functioning amongst the exiles. To him their message, telling of the speedy return of the exiles and therefore inevitably of the fall of Babylon, was treason. So he roasted them, yes, literally! (Jeremiah 29:22) Link this with Daniel chapter three. Maybe it was Nebuchadnezzar's favourite way of dealing with opposition?

❧

By contrast Jeremiah had sent a letter to the exiles giving them the unwelcome news that the exile would be long, around seventy years. So they must settle down and make the best of it. They should build houses, plant gardens so they could eat their produce, marry and settle down to family life. Also they must seek the welfare of Babylon, because only as they did so would they flourish. But most of all, away from temple and all that was familiar, they must seek the Lord Who wanted to be found by them. It would appear that they were free to do all the things Jeremiah instructed. They were living in a compact community, rather than spread out all over the empire as Assyria's captives had been. There is no evidence that they were harshly treated by the Babylonians, but they were exiles torn away from their homeland, and that was trauma enough.

So Ezekiel started his ministry in exile, while all his hearers knew that Jerusalem was still standing. The message of the false prophets was just what the exiles wanted to hear. But Ezekiel's message ran totally counter to that. One can summarise the first twenty four chapters of Ezekiel in four words; quite simply, "Jerusalem has had it!"

As a would-be priest, Ezekiel recoiled in horror from the pollution of Judah's worship by Canaanite rites and practices. The land, the city and the temple had been defiled by these and so he saw the Glory of the Lord leaving the temple. Thus Judah had lost her protection. So Ezekiel sought to communicate with his fellow exiles the fact that Jerusalem herself would be ransacked.

Ezekiel too has oracles against the nations, especially Egypt, on whom Judah too readily depended as an ally and who never in fact came up with the goods. Tyre, the centre of 'world' trade also comes in for an impassioned oracle of judgement.

Eventually, about four months after the Fall of Jerusalem in 586 BC had actually happened, a fugitive from the broken city came to Ezekiel with this news. From now on his task was to build up the faith of a shattered people. Ezekiel saw that God would take the initiative, giving His people a new heart and a new spirit so that they would be able to obey Him. They had been led astray by false shepherds, kings who had gone into syncretism and had not cared for the welfare of their people. (In the Old Testament the shepherd of the people is the king, not the pastor!)

Now God Himself would become their shepherd. The exiles would be restored to their own land. God would act, not for their sake, but for the sake of His Holy Name, His character and reputation which His people had defiled by their behaviour. In this sense He could only vindicate Himself by renewing His people and enabling them to reflect His character. Like God, like people. That principle always works , whether we like it or not. But it works according to our deep emotional perception of God rather than our correct doctrine. The problem for many of the Jews before the Fall of Jerusalem was that they had become like the Baals in character!

Ezekiel had a vision of a the ground plan of new temple. Maybe it is important to point out here that what Ezekiel sees is already before him. He measures it up and describes it in detail, but nowhere is he told it is to be a blueprint for anything which should be in the future. Maybe it symbolises how which the life of Judah should centre around her Holy God in a way which gave due regard to that holiness?

# The Fall of Jerusalem: 2 Kings 25, Lamentations, Psalm 137

AT THE TIME WHEN EZEKIEL had been taken to Babylon in 597BC, Jehoiachin's young uncle was made puppet king of Jerusalem, with the throne name Zedekiah. He was a weak character, quite unable to guide Judah through these critical times, as he was afraid of some of those surrounding him and so was too easily led by them. He often listened to Jeremiah, but never actually took his advice.

Men around Zedekiah urged rebellion to free Judah from the Babylonian yoke. That had about as much chance of success as if one isolated English county declared war on the United States. Jerusalem endured a terrible eighteen month siege in 587/6 BC when some of the starving people even became cannibals. Zedekiah's sons were killed and then he was blinded and taken to Babylon.

❧

In the city itself the temple, palaces, city walls and houses of any importance were destroyed. More Jews were taken to Babylon as exiles. Gedaliah, the son of Ahikam, was appointed by the Babylonians as governor over what remained of Judah and he set up his headquarters at

Mizpah. Presumably Jerusalem was too devastated to be used for this purpose.

Pause to imagine the impact of the exile on the Jews. They had believed that their city would be protected come what may. Never mind what Jeremiah said to the contrary. God needed the temple and the Davidic dynasty... well for the many who thought so, this helped to convince them that He would not let these things go. For too many their religious belief and practice had become a sort of insurance policy. As to what really mattered, faith leading to covenant obedience, well that went out of the window years ago.

In the Ancient Near East the fortunes of a people and their god were closely inter-twined. If the people were defeated in the way Judah had been, that showed that the god really was not up to much as clearly he could not even look after his own. So they might as well look to the stronger gods of their captors. Yet the prophets had maintained that the Lord allowed Judah's defeat, not because of any weakness on His part, for He is Lord of Creation and Lord of the nations. The defeat came as His judgement on His erring people. Maybe, humanly speaking, these prophetic messages saved the faith of Judah in this crisis.

Lamentations shows us the state to which the inhabitants of Jerusalem were reduced during and after the siege of the city. It reveals something of the shock and trauma of the situation. The Jews viewed what happened with blank unbelief: this simply could not be.

Even the kings of other nations did not believe that Jerusalem would fall in this way. Cannibalism had broken out in the starving city during the siege. But life in Jerusalem just after its fall was little better, with people struggling to find food and water.

The author of Lamentations pours his grief into a tightly disciplined series of poems. Further he squarely faces the fact that Judah had brought this on herself because of her wrongdoing in forsaking God. God had done what He had said He would do. So He was still to be trusted. And because He could be trusted there was hope. The basis for this hope, as prophets before him had made clear, was the character of God. It is ever so. The Lord, the God of steadfast love, perseveres with His people.

⋘

Yes, the words of the prophets no doubt saved the faith of Judah in this crisis. The unthinkable had happened. But somewhere both in the memory of the people and also in written scrolls was the fact that prophet after prophet had warned of this. It was not all one great accident. It was the consequence of covenant disobedience. Obedience would have brought blessing, but obedience had been in remarkably short supply. Disobedience brought the curses of the covenant to which Israel had agreed. She had qualified for this by her behaviour long ago, but God had repeatedly let her begin again. Now she was at the point when nothing else but the pain of exile would cure her of her idolatry.

Psalm 137 reveals the raw feeling of exiles from Judah to Babylon. They had suffered horribly during the siege of Jerusalem. How they would have loved to see someone get hold of the Babylonian babies and bash their brains out! The good thing is that this feeling was both acknowledged and expressed in the only safe direction in which it could be expressed, that is, to God.

⋘

Gedaliah, son of Ahikam, was a moderate and wise man and may well have made a good governor for what was left of Judah. Older members of his family, that is the family of Ahikam's father, Shaphan, consistently appear on the side of reform in the time of Jeremiah. But Gedaliah was assassinated not long after his appointment. This meant that those in Judah who had any leadership role now feared Babylonian reprisals and so they fled to Egypt, taking with them the prophet Jeremiah and Baruch, his secretary and companion. So an unorthodox Jewish community flourished in Egypt for some while and these Jews even built their own temple at Elephantine. The Babylonians did take a few more people from Judah into exile around 582 BC.

Hard though it was, the Jews certainly benefited from the exile. It did, in the end, cure them of idolatry once for all. That was never the problem in post-exilic Judaism. It was a great advantage that they were apparently able to live in a fairly compact community. As time passed they began to emphasise everything that made them different from others: their law, the Sabbath, circumcision, food laws. They also began meeting together to worship and read their Scriptures and this is thought to be the beginning of the synagogue movement.

# The Return from Exile: Ezra, Haggai and Zechariah, Esther.

ALMOST SEVENTY YEARS AFTER DANIEL and his friends had been taken into exile, but something under fifty or sixty years for many of those in the later groups of exiles, Babylon fell to a Persian conqueror, Cyrus. It was a surprisingly unbloody conquest in 539BC. Cyrus' policy with captive peoples was to allow them to return to their own country, to encourage them to worship their own gods properly, even if this meant Persian help in financing the building of a temple for them. Of course Cyrus would expect them to remain loyal to Persia and pay their taxes. He would also expect them to pray for him to all the various gods around his empire. Surely some of them should be able to do him some good! So he issued a decree allowing the Jews in his empire to return to Judah and Jerusalem to live. They were to rebuild their temple and he returned most of the temple treasure which the Babylonians had looted earlier. This did not include the Ark of the Covenant. What became of that no-one knows, so the field is open for wild guesswork and speculation of which there has been no shortage! I wonder, had the gold been melted down and then placed in Babylonian coffers?

The book of Ezra covers two distinct periods. The first six chapters do not mention Ezra and it is unlikely that he was even born when the events they record took place as they conclude almost sixty years before he appears on the scene. These six chapters are concerned with this decree of Cyrus, with the return of many Jewish exiles to Jerusalem and with the rebuilding of the temple. Once the foundations were in place and the altar of burnt offering set up, then the Jews could and did re-instate the sacrificial system which had been in abeyance while they had no temple.

It would seem that the returnees made a good start on the building, then concentrated on their own homes and experienced several years of poor crops. Gradually the temple building lapsed. God raised up two prophets, Haggai and Zechariah and they stirred up the Jews to return to the temple building project. New administrators in the area wondered whether what was going on had official Persian permission and so they wrote back to Persia to check that this project really did have royal approval. The new king, Darius made it clear that he was following the same policy as Cyrus. So the temple was completed by 515B.C.

The story told in the book of Esther most likely comes from this period, in between chapters 6 and 7 of the book of Ezra! Here the Persian king, Ahasuerus/Xerxes is the one before the Artaxerxes with whom Ezra and Nehemiah had dealings. After much feasting and display of his wealth, Ahasuerus gave a banquet lasting seven days at which wine flowed freely. Then he ordered his queen, Vashti, to come into the banquet so he could display her beauty to those present. Judging from the likely state of the king and those around him, one can hardly blame Vashti for refusing. Any decent woman would have done the same!

However, this refusal didn't go down too well and she was demoted from being queen, which meant that there was now a vacancy. This didn't mean that the king's harem was suddenly empty! Beautiful girls from around the empire were sought. Each was given twelve months' beauty treatment before a night with the king. If he was not too pleased she went on into the harem. Eventually the king's choice of a replacement for Vashti fell on Esther, a Jewess, who had been brought up by her relative, Mordecai.

As a Jew, Mordecai refused to bow down to Haman, an honoured royal official. Affronted by this, Haman plotted to get rid, not only of Mordecai, but of all the Jews. He persuaded Ahasuerus that these were a people in his empire who followed different customs and did not obey the king's laws and the best thing to do would be to exterminate them. So Ahasuerus signed a decree which would be the death warrant of the Jews in his empire. Mercifully, the date for their destruction was not until the end of the year.

Mordecai persuaded Esther to petition the king for the life of their people. But even Ahasuerus could not revoke his decree. All he could do was pass another decree giving the Jews full permission to defend themselves on the fateful date, which they did very successfully, killing those who would have killed them.

The book of Esther does not mention God. The only whiffs of Jewish religion that we can pick up from it are Mordecai's refusal to bow down to a man and the proclamation of a fast, which we assume was accompanied by prayer. Then there is Mordecai's famous word to Esther in 4:14 showing a clear belief in the providential ordering of affairs. Yet one only has to read through the book to see numerous co-incidences. God may not be centre stage, but He is everywhere active behind the scenes, watching over His people.

❧

The actual story, like the rest of the Old Testament, is far better than I have told it, but then the purpose of this book is to encourage you to read that book, the Old Testament, for yourself.

≪∞

In the middle of the next century the Persian ruler was still concerned that worship should be properly carried out by his subject peoples. Now among those Jewish exiles still in Babylon there was a priest-scribe named Ezra. He was charged with the task of going to Judah and seeing that the people there were properly instructed in their law. In modern jargon, Ezra's appointment would be to a position something like Minister of State for Religious Affairs in Judah.

So Ezra with a number of other Jews undertook the four month journey around the Fertile Crescent and, in answer to his prayers, arrived safely in Jerusalem. They had turned down the king's offer of an armed escort.

Ezra's arrival in Jerusalem was most probably about 458 BC, that is, about eighty years after the first batch of returnees had begun settling down in Jerusalem. These had begun with some fervour to keep the law of Moses. But as the years passed some became lax, especially over the subject of marriage outside the faith. So, to his horror, Ezra found Jews married to women from the tribes surrounding Judah, and children who could only speak their mother's language and not that of the Jews.

This was a very serious situation because the Jewish community was such a small one with a total population not much more than the current population of one of our market towns, say Bury St. Edmunds or Hereford for example. So if the Jewish race continued to be diluted in this way, it could, in the not too distant future, lose its distinctiveness and cease to exist. Further this inter-marriage was a threat to the Jewish religion. We do not read that it had led to outright idolatry and syncretism at this point, but these things were waiting again not too far down this road. The preservation of the faith of Israel at this time depended on maintaining the purity of the Jewish community and Ezra knew that. If that were lost then the foundation on which the Christian faith was yet to be built went with it!

Ezra spent time mourning and fasting and praying. Then he summoned those who had married foreign wives and cases were dealt with one by one. The foreign wives were to be divorced and they and their children were to be sent away. These were drastic measures for a critical situation. In those days of extended families, it is likely that many of those sent away were able to take refuge back in their parental home or with others in their extended families.

❧

Here again to use the term 'ethnic cleansing' would be misleading. It is important in this connection to note that no-one's life was in danger and that alone makes this term unsuitable. But there is also the important fact that the root concern was for the faith of Israel. That was in danger of being lost altogether if this inter-marriage had gone on unchecked.

It has been said that Judah went into exile a nation and came back a church. What this means was that up until the time of exile, Judah had her own king and some sort of national autonomy, even though she had been very much under Babylonian domination for the dozen years or so before the Fall of Jerusalem in 586 BC. But when the Jews returned from exile, Judah remained part of the Persian Empire. There was no question of the Jews being allowed to run their own affairs. Empires might still come and go as indeed they did, but such changes did not bring political freedom to the Jews. In fact they had only a very brief period of independence before the time of Christ. By that time they had lost this independence again and they were, of course, part of the Roman

Empire. But Judah was a distinct religious community. So the faith of Judah had been preserved.

# The End of the Old Testament: Nehemiah and Malachi

AROUND 445 BC A DEPUTATION of Jews from Jerusalem arrived at the court of Artaxerxes II of Persia. In particular they spoke to a Jew named Nehemiah who was in the trusted position of being the king's cup-bearer. So it was his job to see that the king didn't get poisoned and, in doing the job he would be glad to avoid this fate himself! He appears to have been successful on both these counts.

The news these Jews brought caused Nehemiah great distress and anguish. It was that the walls of Jerusalem had been thrown down and its gates burned with fire. Now every Jew knew about the destruction of Jerusalem in 586B.C. and now, one hundred and forty years later, though this was an on-going source of pain for the Jews, it certainly would not have accounted for Nehemiah's grief. For a parallel we don't get that upset about say British losses in the Crimean War. Perhaps the bombing of London in the blitz in the Second World War is a better example and yet it would be astonishing if even that produced grief in us today like this news did for Nehemiah.

In Ezra 4:7-23 we read of an abortive attempt by the Jews to rebuild the walls of Jerusalem without official Persian permission early in the reign of this Artaxerxes, Nehemiah's boss. Local officials had informed Artaxerxes of this and he had ordered that the illegal work be demolished. So it was almost certainly this much more recent news, previously unknown to Nehemiah, that his brother, Hanani, brought to him. Jerusalem was not secure. Besides this, the broken down walls would be a source of disgrace.

No doubt the Jewish delegation were looking to Nehemiah for help. If anything at all was to happen then Nehemiah had to ask Artaxerxes for a U-turn in policy towards Jerusalem. Absolute rulers are not used to complying with such requests! There could even be nasty consequences for the petitioner. No wonder Nehemiah prayed and fasted for months before speaking to Artaxerxes. In fact, he only did so when Artaxerxes noticed that he looking sad and asked him the reason for this. Nehemiah boldly took this opportunity, asking for permission to go to Jerusalem and oversee the repair of the city walls, for letters of safe conduct and also for the materials he knew he would need for the project. Unlike Ezra, he accepted the armed escort provided by the King for his journey.

The established officials, Sanballat and Tobiah in the province of Trans-Euphrates of which Judah was now but a small part, were very put out that someone should come with authority to improve the condition of Jerusalem. After all this was in their patch and they had no great love for it! They were out to make as much trouble as they could and were quite inventive in the ways they did this. Occasionally they had Geshem the Arab with them as a fellow conspirator.

On arriving at Jerusalem, Nehemiah did a night time inspection of the damage to the walls. Then he called together the people of Jerusalem and reminded them of their unprotected situation, telling them of the way in which God had answered his prayers resulting in Artaxerxes' willingness now to allow the walls to be repaired. So he urged them to join him in repairing the walls and, by the time he ended his speech, they were ready to begin building.

Nehemiah then allocated different sections of wall to different groups, very often assigning people the task of repairing the wall near their own house. That would mean that they would work with enthusiasm and do a good job! He knew how to get the best out of people.

Sanballat and company charged them with rebellion against the Persian King, ridiculed their efforts, made plans to attack them by night and tried several times to kidnap Nehemiah. It took great perseverance on his part to counter these threats and to encourage the Jews to stick at the job for the couple of months until the walls and gates were completely repaired. It was evident even to the Jews' enemies that God had been helping them in this work.

Gatekeepers were appointed and the gates kept shut throughout all the hours of darkness, once again giving Jerusalem the normal protection of a walled city. At the beginning of the seventh month Ezra read from the Book of the Law to the assembled Jews, while Levites were appointed to make the meaning clear to the hearers. Thus great care was taken to ensure that the Law was understood. Many Jews wept as they heard the words of the Law, but were told to celebrate the festival day to the Lord. Certainly many rejoiced now that they understood the Law. After this, the Feast of Booths or Tabernacles was celebrated. This marked the end of the agricultural year and was an eight day period during which those attending were to live in leafy booths made out of branches of trees. Later the same month there was another great gathering for reading the Law, confessing sin and praising God.

After this the priests, Levites and leaders made a binding agreement that they would follow the Law of Moses. In particular they would not inter-marry with those of other races, and would see that all the duties connected with running the temple were faithfully fulfilled.

During his governorship Nehemiah had dealt with some social problems in Jerusalem caused by the greed of the nobility who had been lending money at interest. We take interest on loans for granted, but remember that in those days people only borrowed because they were desperate for something to eat. It would be all they could do to repay the original loan and that is why the lending at interest was forbidden. So Nehemiah shamed the nobles into giving back property which had been mortgaged to them and into leaving off interest charges. He himself set a good example by not aking the governor's allowance to which he was entitled, so as not to be a burden on the ordinary people.

After a twelve year stint in Jerusalem Nehemiah was recalled to Persia, but managed to come back to Jerusalem a bit later on. He found much to displease him in the laxity which had crept into the city, which he sought to rectify with his usual abrasive vigour.

The final book in your Old Testament is the book of the prophet Malachi. This is about the last we hear of the little Jewish community and what we find here is not very promising. The fervour of the returnees has certainly worn thin by now. Both priests and people had become lax in both worship and life. Malachi warns that the Lord will act in purifying judgement. But by contrast, there is also mention of people who did love God, who kept in close contact with each other and of whose devotion the Lord had taken note.

# Poetic Books:
## Job, Psalms, Proverbs, Ecclesiastes, Song of Songs.

THE PRINTING OF OLD TESTAMENT in modern Bible translations makes clear that some of it is in prose and some in poetry. The way in which Hebrew poetry works is rather different from our way of doing it, but conveniently it is not so easily lost in translation as English poetry would be.

Hebrew poetry is usually built up in one of three ways.

An idea is first expressed and then it is repeated in different words: these may add a richness to the meaning, but essentially the same thing is being said twice. Psalm 2:1-3 illustrates this quite well.

Or an idea may be expressed and then it is immediately followed by its opposite as in Psalm 1:6. You will find five examples in Proverbs 28:1-6. Can you spot which verse is the odd one out here?

The third device used frequently is for an idea first to be expressed and then to be built up in the next two or three lines. Psalm 1:1,3,4-5 are good examples of this.

৯

Job is one of a few books of the Old Testament written almost entirely in poetry except, in this case, for the first two chapters and the final one.

The story is located in the land of Uz, wherever that was. The atmosphere is patriarchal. One feels Abraham would have been quite at home in the culture and worship reflected here.

Job is a prosperous man whose whole life is patterned by his faith in God. In Job 1-2, the prose prologue, Satan, the adversary, makes one of his three public appearances in the Old Testament. He challenges God, saying that Job's piety is only cupboard love, and will soon evaporate if God allows him to take away Job's goods and family. When Job survives this first test with his faith intact, then Satan asks for permission to test Job further by inflicting severe illness upon him. He is allowed to do this so long as Job's life is spared.

Job's three friends, Eliphaz, Bildad and Zophar come and see him. For a week they sit with him in silence and in that way their presence may well have been a comfort to Job. It is when they open their mouths and try to explain what has happened to him from the viewpoint of their limited theology that trouble begins. Perhaps there is a lesson for us here.

For the friends have a firm belief that all suffering is the result of sin. Great sin produces great suffering. The logical reverse of that is that great suffering results from great sin. Job is suffering greatly, therefore Job has sinned greatly. Q.E.D.

The three vary in the delicacy or bluntness with which they state this. They each speak in turn, with Job replying to each speech. One round, two rounds and then in the third round Eliphaz had his turn, Bildad falters, (someone suggested he had run out of gas,) and Zophar has already said what he meant pointedly enough and does not participate further.

In reply Job refutes these charges and labels his friends as miserable comforters, worthless physicians who have no understanding of his situation. Part of his responses are aimed at his friends, but increasingly he appears to lose sight of them and to address his questions to God. Don't think of Job as quiet and submissive. He speaks frankly to God about the confusion, agony and turmoil he feels and his sense that God is treating him unjustly.

After the great appeal for God's wisdom in chapter 28, Job outlines first his honoured position in the community before this crisis, then the contrast with his miserable situation now, followed by an affirmation of his way of life, showing a care for the less fortunate and a concern to keep even his thought life pure. This portrays a very warm and likeable picture of the godly life in Old Testament times.

After all this a young man, Elihu, has his say, but he does not contribute a great deal that is new to the argument. Finally God himself speaks to Job, not to answer his questions for He does not go in for that, but to reveal His greatness. But meeting with God like this satisfies Job in a way which answered questions never could have done. Job's prosperity is restored as this was necessary for his vindication to be recognised in that culture.

❧

Is the book, as is usually supposed, about the problem of innocent suffering, or is it about the crisis of faith, about the challenge to the sufferer's relationship with God which such suffering can produce especially when it is faced with a rigid and inappropriate doctrine as to why it has occurred? The answer is probably a bit of both.

This is a book which has brought comfort to many in all sorts of life crises. It encourages an open relationship with God, where whatever we think or feel may be shared with Him.

After Job is the book of Psalms somewhere around the middle of our Bibles. These may well span the period of the monarchy and beyond. They are essentially a response to God in prayer and praise, adoration and worship. In them the worshipper also expresses his despair and hope, his hatreds and his fears, his anxieties and his joys. He is open to God about them all. Some psalms are given a link with specific occasions, but the language is sufficiently general for them to be of use to us and to fit in with our 'occasions' whatever these may be. This generality helps to give the psalms their constant value We could find a psalm to fit our mood or needs on any day. Many of them are suitable for either public or private use.

Psalms 1, 19 and 119 in particular express delight in God's law, detailing some of the benefits it brings into the life of one who loves it and abides by it. Too many people see God's law as restrictive. Not so the psalmist: he had the right idea. In fact God's law is protective. It is intended to be a fence around us, preventing us from harming ourselves and others. Within these boundaries are light and life, beyond them darkness and death.

In other psalms God is seen to be the security of His people. He is a rock, refuge, stronghold, fortress and deliverer. Much is made of His steadfast love, His covenant love towards His people, His faithfulness in all sorts of circumstances and His loving kindness and mercy and willingness to forgive. Several psalms show an awareness that the author has sinned and Psalm 51 in particular, is a confession of sin and plea for God's mercy.

A number of psalms speak of crises in life which often take one of two forms. One is severe illness or some other event which brings the psalmist face to face with death. In all of these except for psalm 88, the gloom is lifted and the psalm goes on to record either the way in which God has responded to prayer or strong confidence that He will do so.

But the second strand in the psalms is one which we, in our comfortable life-style in the West, do not always know what to do with. It is the prayers about, and against, the psalmists' enemies. These appear numerous, the enemies I mean, and they pop up where one is not expecting them. They are often life threatening too. The psalmists' reaction to them is not what we would always feel free to express in Christian circles. Does that really mean we don't sometimes feel what the psalmist expresses here?

I guess these psalms dealing with the enemies have enormous value for the many thousands of our Christian brothers and sisters who live in the parts of the world where today they are constantly persecuted for their faith in Christ. And if they find their initial reaction to such enemies is a sub-Christian one, then here is an invitation to pour it out to God, to be open with Him about it. That is step one to sorting it out.

The psalms also celebrate God's kingship over creation and over the nations and over Israel. It's worth praying to Him because He is in a position to act. All power is His. He hasn't got tied and tangled up in His own creation as some seem to suppose!

It was the faith held by Israelites in Old Testament times which produced the psalms. Here are outpourings of worship, thanksgiving, adoration and praise to which the Christian Church constantly turns to express her own sense of gratitude to, and also her love for, God.

Proverbs is a collection of wise sayings, observations about life and the way it normally works. This is the kind of wisdom for which Solomon was famous and considerable sections of the book are attributed to him.

Wisdom is extolled and is to be sought above all else. Wily women are to be resisted: the consequences of not doing so are painted quite vividly as a needful warning. Diligence is commended and the sluggard lampooned. There is advice on how to conduct oneself prudently in all manner of ordinary life situations. A great deal is said about the use of the tongue for good or ill. Piety is commended and the fear of the Lord is the beginning of wisdom. One can gain a great deal from meditating on these wise sayings and putting them into practice.

❦

Ecclesiastes is a strangely modern book. The author explores the futility of life bounded by death and this world. What is the point of life if death ends it? The things of this world, wealth, wisdom, wine and women fail to satisfy the craving heart of man, and even hard work won't do it either. Further, life is not fair and nothing is guaranteed, except that life will end in death.

What is best to do in this situation? It is important to fear God and obey Him. It is also good to enjoy the present moment and to do whole heartedly whatever one might have to do.

Though I am not aware of anyone managing to extract any Messianic prophecy out of Ecclesiastes, this is a book which screams out for a New Testament and for its certainty about eternal life and thus purpose in this life.

❦

The Song of Songs extols erotic love! After all, it was God's idea, part of His good creation. God's plan and intention is that this should be expressed and enjoyed within the safeguards of marriage, which should be a faithful, committed, stable relationship. As you read this book you will notice how what was complimentary in the culture of the time the Song of Songs was written would hardly go down well nowadays. If you tell your beloved that her nose is like a tower of Lebanon, she may not feel flattered, whether or not you add that it looks towards Damascus. (Song of Songs 7:4)

Over the centuries the church, which has often had difficulties in accepting the right use of sex as one of God's great gifts, has never quite been able to stomach the plain meaning of this book. So it has been taken as an allegory of the love between God and Israel or Christ and the Church. You can extract quite a bit of blessing from it by reading it in that way as a sort of allegory, but I challenge anyone to find a single indication within the text that that is what it was intended to be.

# *Thoughts on the Value of the Old Testament Itself.*

Some of the revelations of the nature of God shown in the Old Testament are simply assumed in the New Testament. They are not repeated there and you can fail to pick them up if you try to limit your self to the New Testament.

One of the questions which students on a Correspondence Course with the London School of Theology used to answer was, 'What impact has your study of the Old Testament had on your Christian faith?' Time and again one important aspect of this answer was that by reading the Old Testament, the reader's concept of God had grown. He was so much bigger than they had ever imagined! Mind you, none of us have grasped anything like the full extent of His power and His love.

This impact is partly due to the revelation of God as Creator. In the Old Testament He does not merely create the world and then sit back and watch it get on with it! No, the whole lot works because He makes it work. The grass grows because He makes it grow. If He didn't, it wouldn't. Think of that next time you complain about having to cut the lawn! A number of times in the Old Testament we see God use His Creation to do His bidding.

Further He is revealed as Lord of History, King of the Nations. We see His purposes fulfilled even by pagan kings. So Assyria is the rod of his anger (Isaiah 10:5) and the great conquests of which the Assyrian boasted were only what God had planned long before (Isaiah 37:26-29). Nebuchadnezzar of Babylon is called 'My servant' (Jeremiah 27:6) as he unwittingly carries out God's judgement on idolatrous Judah. It may be decidedly dodgy nowadays to say precisely what God is doing on the international scene, but we can be quite confident that He is in charge. He knows what He is doing. If we are sure of that, do we have to know too? What we do need is to be sure of Him, to know in our hearts that He is to be trusted.

Thus the Old Testament anchors us in God amidst all the turmoil of this world. He is in charge. He has not abdicated. After all, there is no point in praying to a god who is not in charge. But then, such would be no god.

There are great devotional riches in the Old Testament. The psalms are unsurpassed in Scripture for their outpourings of praise, thanksgiving, adoration and worship. So this is the expression of the spiritual life of Israelites living during what could often look like dark days. If only we could learn to praise God like they did!

In the Old Testament we have the opportunity to see characters develop in their relationship with God. We see how Joseph grows and changes through the hardships he undergoes. God trains Moses for a very special task. You could read through Judges 6-7 to see how Gideon's faith in God develops. All these and so many more, are opportunities for us to learn about God's dealings with us. We have less opportunity to study God's dealings with individuals in the New Testament since the events there cover a period of not a lot more than fifty or so years against the Old Testament's fifteen hundred years.

Thus we read of God's dealings with nations over a long period. We watch the great empires parade for a while over the stage of history in their pomp and pride and we see the outcome of this. That can encourage us in our own times.

The Old Testament lays the foundations laid for most of the concepts we will find in New Testament

When you read through the New Testament you will find that the prayers in it are very polite. You probably would expect them to be. But have you noticed that this cannot be said of many of the prayers of the Old Testament? Here people do let off steam to God, however they are feeling. They say it like they feel it. 'God, why haven't you done this, that, or the other?' 'I keep calling to you and you don't take any notice. Have you gone deaf?'. 'The way you run this world of yours isn't fair!' Well, those are a few of the sentiments expressed.

What many Old Testament prayers show is that people had no inhibitions at all about speaking to God just as they felt. They knew they could be totally honest with God. They also knew it was fruitless to be anything else. This kind of talk is the fruit of a strong relationship. You will find it particularly in Job, Psalms and Jeremiah, but not exclusively there.

So the Old Testament invites us to open the whole of our lives up to God, the darker places as well as the sunny ones. For many people nowadays that would be a leap forward.

# The Old Testament Looks Forward to the New Testament.

I HAVE CONSTANTLY FELT THAT so many Christians are impoverished by their regarding the Old Testament merely as a mine of proof texts for the New Testament. Even when we are dealing with just some of the ways in which the Old Testament looks forward to the New Testament, we would do well to get away from the idea of proof texts. The whole subject is so much bigger than that.

The entire cultic system of the Old Testament, that is the way the Israelites worshipped God, priesthood, sacrifices, tabernacle/temple and annual festivals, finds its fulfilment in Christ. He is the great High Priest, Who not only enters the presence of God with the blood of the sacrifice, in this case His own, but opens that way for all believers. When Jesus died the veil, the curtain of the Temple, which excluded even the ordinary priests on duty from the Holy of Holies, was torn in two from top to bottom, showing that the way into the presence of God is now open to us. Our reading of the Old Testament should impress upon us what an enormous privilege this is.

The sacrificial system of the Old Testament prepares and educates us for the sacrifice of Christ. Without it we would be unable to interpret the death of Christ for us. What sense could we make of it as 'for us' if we were totally ignorant of everything in the Old Testament?

One way of appreciating more what Christ has done for us at the cross would be to study the sacrificial system in Leviticus 1-7 and be aware of both its cost and its limitations. Then we would see what Paul means in Acts 13:38-39.

Jesus Himself valued the Old Testament law (Matthew 5:17-20). His conflict with the Pharisees was not about that. It was about the Tradition of the Elders. Let me explain what that was and how it arose. Just under two hundred years before Christ came, the Syrian ruler of the Eastern Mediterranean lands, Antiochus IV, had wanted to unite all his people in common Greek beliefs and culture. Only the Jews stood out against this, or at least some of the Jews. They were the Hasidim, the Covenant Ones, who were prepared to face death rather than compromise their faith. In the end, at great cost, they won through and humanly speaking, it was due to them that the faith of Israel was preserved at that time.

Some of the spiritual descendants of the Hasidim became the Pharisees. So intent were they on preserving and keeping the law, that they wrote around it numerous petty regulations which were intended to define it, but ended up in killing its spirit completely. For example they had over twenty regulations around the law on keeping the Sabbath day holy. They had even discussed whether you could eat an egg laid on the Sabbath. Clearly the hen responsible for a Sabbath egg had not been hot on sabbath observance! These rules and regulations which the Pharisees had woven around the law were known as the Tradition of the Elders. Jesus' frequent disputes with the Pharisees centred on the Tradition of the Elders, the attempt to define the law in rigid rules and petty regulations.

In the Old Testament there are prophecies concerning the coming of the Prophet like Moses in Deuteronomy 18, the Suffering Servant of Isaiah, the Son of Man in Daniel and the Messiah descended from David in various passages from the time of David onwards. Messiah means 'Anointed One' and it applied to the descendant of David whose coming was foretold. In the prophecy of Isaiah, the Suffering Servant is not identified with the Messiah, nor is the Messiah identified with Daniel's Son of Man. It is Jesus who combines these lines of thought as He fulfils them all in Himself. I think we will understand them more if we are willing to see them as they are, separate in the Old Testament, but combined in the New.

Then there is the incompleteness of the Old Testament What happens after this life?

There is no great clarity on that one, though there are a number of hints and aspirations. There is the general idea that the dead go to Sheol, a dull grey half life, beyond God's care, a prospect to be avoided as long as possible. Here and there individuals see beyond that. Job certainly does not in chapter 14, but he may do in chapter 19. Whether the endings to Psalms 16 and 73 said as much to their original readers as we Christians often find in them is a moot point, but there are hints in the Old Testament pointing to something better than Sheol. Here and there one can find a statement which can only mean resurrection, such is Daniel 12:2, but it would be difficult to construct firm doctrine on just a few verses. Thank God that the situation on this vital issue is so different in the New Testament which speaks with such certainty about resurrection and eternal life.

The covenants of the Old Testament with Noah and with Abraham worked well enough as these made few demands on humanity. But the Sinai covenant, which offered such blessing to Israel, also declared curses for disobedience and Israel experienced these. Jeremiah foretold a new covenant. This would be different. It would work positively. It would start in the only place a relationship with God can start, with full and free forgiveness. Those within this covenant would be able to keep it as God would write His law in their hearts and minds, giving them the will and desire and power to walk in it. They would belong to Him and be His people and He would be their God. They would know Him in a living relationship. This new and better covenant was brought into being by the death of Christ. Luke 22:20, Hebrews 8:7-13. It is this new covenant which gives its name to this part of our Bibles: New Testament.

Such a God Who is Lord of human history would find His way to bless all peoples. For as we have seen, He is Lord of the nations. But from the beginning He was working out His plan to share His blessings, the knowledge of Himself, with all peoples. For His original promise to Abraham was that through his descendants all peoples of the earth would be blessed. Jesus was a descendant of Abraham, born amidst other descendants of Abraham and, however many disbelieved, yet there were enough who followed Christ for the good news of His salvation to be spread around the known world within a generation.

The Old Testament, with its rich revelation of God, with its promises and God-given insights is ours in Christ. Because of Him, we can benefit from all that it has to say. Remember, it was His Bible! So it must be worthwhile getting to know it.

God may speak to us in many ways. One regular way in which He speaks is through the Bible, through any part of the Bible. There is only one way to get to know what He wants to say to you through different parts of the Old Testament. Read it for yourself. Then go on reading it. You won't exhaust what it contains and what He has to say to you. You will miss all this if you neglect it.

All the current translations of the Bible into English go back to the original Hebrew of the Old Testament and Greek of the New Testament and each is an attempt to put this anew into English. The correct name for such a translation is a version. Find a version that suits you and get down to it.

I suggest that you may find the New Living Translation of the Bible a good one to start on as you read the Old Testament. It is a very clear translation, I am tempted to say, clearer than the original in places! But it's a really good read and so I heartily commend it to you.

You may well find the idea of reading straight through the Old Testament far too daunting. Just go for a book at a time. There is no need to begin at Genesis and plough straight through. Choose any book. Make sure you understand where it fits into the whole. Read it at whatever pace suits you. Get a grip on its content and message. That may take more than one reading. Then you will be ready to go on to another book. The only way to get to know the Bible is to read it a book at a time. No, I am not saying a book at a sitting, though that is easy with some of the very short ones. But stick with one book till you feel you know it a bit.

❧

My prayer is that you will enjoy the whole Bible, the Old Testament as well as the New Testament and, through this, grow in the knowledge of Jesus Christ as Saviour and Lord, Companion and Friend throughout your life. For the whole purpose of reading and knowing the Bible is that we may know Him in a living relationship.

# *Putting*
# *The Old Testament Together*

2000 BC **Abraham,**
followed by Isaac, then **Jacob/Israel** and his twelve sons, whose descendants became the twelve tribes of Israel..
**The Israelites went into Egypt** to get food and were eventually reduced to slavery

Possibly around 1280 BC **God rescued the Israelites from slavery in Egypt.**
The establishment of the **Sinai Covenant,** the core of which is the Ten Commandments
Forty years in the wilderness between Egypt and Canaan.

**Conquest of Canaan** by Israel under **Joshua.**

The period of the **Judges:** some may have overlapped with others as their sphere of influence was often only a few of the twelve tribes.
Around 1050BC **Samuel** judges the whole of Israel.

Israel asks for a king.
**The United Monarchy** around 1020-921BC

**Saul** in many ways like another of the judges, but with title of king.

## David 1000-960BC

Secured Israel's borders: captured Jerusalem and made it his capital. Made preparations for the building of a temple.

## Solomon 960-921 BC

Inherited secure country from David: built temple. Extravagant building programme and luxurious life-style overtaxed his subjects

## The Divided Kingdom  921-586 BC

921 BC The ten northern tribes, **Israel,** broke away from the house of David and appointed **Jeroboam** as King.
He set up golden calves at centres of worship at **Dan and Bethel** and a religious system which was not in accordance with the law of Moses.

The remaining tribe, Judah and part of Benjamin, called **Judah,** stayed with **Rehoboam,** the son of Solomon. Jerusalem was the capital and the king always descended from David (except Athaliah!)

So we follow the **Northern Kingdom** which lasted until 721 BC

Dynasties were usually short-lived. **All kings followed Jeroboam I's religious system.** This was 'the sin of Jeroboam, the son of Nebat, who made Israel to sin'.

Omri in the ninth century built **Samaria** as his capital.
His son, **Ahab,** married **Jezebel** of Tyre, who promoted the worship of her own form of Baal with missionary zeal in Israel.

God sent his two prophets **Elijah and Elisha** in the ninth century BC to combat this Baal worship.

In the eighth century the prophets **Amos and Hosea** prophesied to Israel to call her back to God. There was no repentance.

721 BC **Assyria conquered Israel.** She settled many Israelites throughout her vast empire and populated Israel with mixed peoples

from various places in her empire. The resulting mixed population living in the northern territory took their name from its capital, Samaria...**the Samaritans,** later despised by pure bred Jews.

### That was the end of the Northern Kingdom.

So we turn to the **Southern Kingdom, Judah.** which lasted till 586BC

Eighth century prophets **Micah and Isaiah** sought to recall the country to faithfulness to God.

701 BC God miraculously rescued Jerusalem from an Assyrian attack led by Sennacherib in the time of Hezekiah.

**Hezekiah** was followed by the long and evil reign of his son, **Manasseh,** whose idolatry sealed Judah's fate.

**Josiah** sought to reverse this idolatrous trend...too late.

627-586+ **Jeremiah** the prophet during the last days of Judah.
612 *Babylonians sacked Nineveh, capital of Assyria*

605BC **Babylonian** attack on Judah: **Daniel** and friends taken to Babylon

598/7 BC Another **Babylonian** attack on Judah and Jerusalem: King **Jehoiachin.** nobles, artisans and soldiers taken into **exile in Babylon** Reign of puppet king, **Zedekiah**, in the last days of Judah. He rebelled against Babylon

**586 BC Babylonians destroyed Jerusalem, temple, palaces, city walls etc. More Jews taken into exile.**

539BC **Cyrus of Persia conquered Babylon:** policy to allow captive people to return home to worship own gods in own lands. **So Jews allowed to return to Jerusalem and rebuild Temple,** which was complete by 515BC after encouragement from the prophets, **Haggai and Zechariah.**

Jews back from exile encouraged to worship God: They had no political freedom. The exile had cured them once for all of idolatry.

458 BC **Ezra** came to Jerusalem to teach the law of God
445 BC **Nehemiah** came to Jerusalem to repair the city walls.
**Malachi,** the latest of the OT prophets fits in about here.

The Old Testament story ends here, over 400 years before the birth of Christ.

Printed in Great Britain
by Amazon.co.uk, Ltd.,
Marston Gate.